750/750

ROMAN THEATER-TEMPLES

PRINCETON MONOGRAPH
IN ART AND ARCHAEOLOGY
XXXIII

✧

PUBLISHED FOR THE
DEPARTMENT OF ART AND ARCHAEOLOGY
PRINCETON UNIVERSITY

ROMAN
THEATER-TEMPLES

BY JOHN ARTHUR HANSON

PRINCETON, NEW JERSEY

PRINCETON UNIVERSITY PRESS

1959

The Library of Congress has cataloged this book as
follows:

Hanson, John Arthur. Roman theater-temples. Princeton, N.J., Princeton University Press, 1959. 124 p. illus.
31 cm. (Princeton monograph in art and archaeology,
33) 1. Theaters—Rome. 2. Temples, Roman. I. Title.
NA325.T5H3 (725.82) 58-13936 ‡ Library of Congress

PRINTED IN THE UNITED STATES OF AMERICA

BY PRINCETON UNIVERSITY PRESS, PRINCETON, N.J.

CONIVGI MEAE

ACKNOWLEDGMENTS

I wish to express my thanks first to Professor Erik Sjöqvist of Princeton University, in whose seminar in Roman topography this study may be said to have begun, and who has patiently encouraged me in the midst of my later wanderings in archaeology. Further thanks are due to Professor Lily Ross Taylor, director of the Classical School of the American Academy in Rome during my stay there from 1953 to 1955, for her encouragement and for her unselfishness in offering me the use of an unpublished paper which I have cited in my discusssions of the temple of Magna Mater and of the *sellisternium*. Dr. Lawrence Richardson, Jr., of Yale and M. Edmond Frézouls of the Bardo Museum in Tunis have both graciously encouraged me to intrude upon their domains. Thanks are due also to Professor George E. Duckworth of Princeton University for his careful reading and kind comments. Not least, I wish to acknowledge my gratitude to Professors Herbert C. Youtie and Frank O. Copley of the University of Michigan.

A few days before this monograph left my hands I had the privilege of examining galley proofs of the new and extensively revised edition of Margarete Bieber's *The History of the Greek and Roman Theater*, and have been able to correct the references which I had made to the first edition of this work. It was impossible to add to my documentation all the references which should now be made to Mrs. Bieber's book, which may serve the reader as a convenient source for bibliography and additional illustrations of many of the Roman theaters discussed here.

The illustrations have been prepared with the help of a grant from the Horace H. Rackham School of Graduate Studies at the University of Michigan. Thanks are due all the publishers who have graciously permitted me to reproduce illustrations. Specific sources are included in the documentation to the discussion of the individual monuments.

JOHN ARTHUR HANSON
Ann Arbor, Michigan
April 1958

CONTENTS

ABBREVIATIONS

AA: Archäologischer Anzeiger

AntCl: L'Antiquité classique

ArchCl: Archeologia Classica

ArchEspArq: Archivo Español de Arqueologia

Atti4CStR: Atti del 4 Congresso Nazionale di Studi Romani

AttiVen: Atti del Reale istituto Veneto di scienze, lettere ed arti

BCH: Bulletin de correspondance hellénique

BdI: Bullettino dell'Istituto di Corrispondenza Archeologica

BSA: British School at Athens, Annual

BullComm: Bullettino della Commisssione Archeologica Communale di Roma

CIL: Corpus Inscriptionum Latinarum

CJ: Classical Journal

CPCP: University of California Publications in Classical Philology

CP: Classical Philology

EphDac: Ephemeris Dacoromana

EphEp: Ephemeris Epigraphica

FA: Fasti Archaeologici

MAAR: Memoirs of the American Academy in Rome

MdI: Mitteilungen der deutschen archäologischen Instituts (1948-)

MélRome: Mélanges d'archéologie et d'histoire de l'École française de Rome

MemLinc: Memorie della R. Accademia Nazionale dei Lincei

NSc: Notizie degli Scavi di Antichità

RA: Revue archéologique

REA: Revue des études anciennes

RE: Pauly-Wissowa, Real-Encyclopädie der klassischen Altertumswissenschaft

RendPontAcc: Atti della Pontificia Accademia Romana di Archeologia, Rendiconti

RevPhil: Revue de philologie, de littérature et d'histoire anciennes

RHist: Revue historique

RM: Mitteilungen des deutschen archäologischen Instituts, Römische Abteilung

RN: Revue numismatique

TAPA: Transactions of the American Philological Association

ThLL: Thesaurus Linguae Latinae

INTRODUCTION

"Ubi sunt ludi scaenici nisi in rebus divinis?" (August. *De civ. D.* vi. 5)

INTRODUCTION

MODERN SCHOLARSHIP has generally characterized the Roman theater of the late Republic and Empire as thoroughly secular. The question of religion has necessarily entered into all discussions of the introduction of theatrical performances into Rome and the significance of Roman *ludi,* including *ludi scaenici.* But the possibility is scarcely mentioned that any trace of this religious connection may have survived into the period when stone theaters were being constructed throughout the Roman world. Many writers have maintained that theaters and shrines were completely separated during the Empire,[1] and only occasionally have scholars contradicted this generalization.[2]

Such was not, however, the view expressed by the church fathers. They do not denounce the theater merely on the grounds that it was a place of immoral conduct, but also because it was inextricably associated with pagan religion.[3] In fact, the central portion of Tertullian's *De Spectaculis* is a demonstration that the games and shows of his time were actually a form of idolatry and should not, therefore, be attended by Christians. His statement that "ex idololatria universam spectaculorum paraturam constare" (*De Spect.* 4. 3) finds close parallels in Arnobius (*Adv. Nat.* vii. 33), Lactantius (*Div. Inst.* vi. 20. 36), Salvianus (*De gubernatione Dei* vi. 11), and Augustine, who quarrels with Varro for not placing his discussion of the theater "in rebus divinis" (*De civ. D.* vi. 3-6). Whatever view one may take of the distortion of fact in early Christian writers, one cannot accuse them of using proofs which would be unacceptable to their contemporaries. They would not, in order to win a point, make unbelievable assertions about phenomena as familiar to their audience as Roman theatrical and circus performances. From their evidence alone, then, one might conclude that the religious associations of the later Roman theater were not as far from the minds of the Romans as they have been from the writings of modern scholars. It is perhaps not without significance that Vitruvius begins his section on the construction of a theater with the mention of the gods: "When the Forum has been laid out, then, for the purpose of watching performances on the holidays of the immortal

[1] E.g., Allardyce Nicoll (*The Development of the Theatre,* p. 50): "The fact remains that the theatre for the Romans was nothing but a theatre; its association with the temple had vanished"; and A. W. Bijvanck ("De theatro antiquo," *Mnemosyne,* XLVIII [1920], 146): "Theatrum Romanum autem nullo modo coniunctum erat cum cultu deorum, sicut theatrum Atticum." Bibliographical data omitted from the notes are supplied in the Bibliography.

[2] E.g., Edmond Frézouls in "Teatri romani dell' Africa francese," *Dioniso,* xv (1952), 100; and Lily Ross Taylor in "Lucretius on the Roman Theatre," *Studies in Honour of Gilbert Norwood,* p. 151. Margarete Bieber has given attention to the recent evidence on this question, and states (*The History of the Greek and Roman Theater,* ch. 14) that the Romans "sometimes built sanctuaries above the uppermost gallery."

[3] This is supported in the article of Lidia Charpin, "Testimonianze christiane sul teatro romano dell'età imperiale," *AttiVen,* xc (1930-31), 571.

gods, a site must be chosen for the theater. . . ."[4] It is further noteworthy that Vergil's allegorical temple to Augustus (*G.* iii. 13-39) has a stage building near it (vv. 24-25).

Tertullian's proofs for the religious nature of *ludi* are preceded by the following subject outline:

> First we shall treat their *origins* one by one, mentioning the rudimentary forms in which they came of age; then the *titles* of some of them, telling the names by which they are known; next the *apparatus* and the superstitions which govern its preparation; then the *sites* and the divinities to whom they are dedicated; and finally the various *skills* of the performers and their reputed inventors.[5]

In the present study of the physical connections which the Roman theater building maintained with religion, only "sites" and "apparatus" will be treated. The religious implications under the other headings are indeed more generally known and accepted:[6] that all *ludi* are in origin religious acts designed in some way to placate the gods;[7] that they are named mainly for divinities and later for the birthdays and accession days of the emperors;[8] that actors and other theatrical workers were sometimes under the patronage of Apollo as "parasiti Apollinis."[9] More may even be known now about *origines*, through the help of anthropology, than Tertullian meant to imply.[10] But the sense in which the *loca* and *apparatus* of the Roman theater may be religious has been insufficiently studied.

The specific example which Tertullian cites under the heading *loca* is the theater of Pompey, at the top of which stood a temple of Venus Victrix. Literary evidence provides no further examples of such an architectural combination, but archaeological evidence can be called in to confirm or deny its uniqueness. The only person seriously to maintain that the theater of Pompey was not *sui generis*—an architectural sport—is Dorothy Kent Hill, who has suggested that it may form part of a consistent architectural tradition.[11] She has briefly recorded some of its possible ancestors and descend-

---

[4] "Cum forum constitutum fuerit, tum deorum immortalium diebus festis ludorum spectationibus elegendus est locus theatro." (v. 3. 1) The gods appear at the beginning of the clause in the Latin.

[5] "Commemorabimus *origines* singulorum, quibus in cunabulis in saeculo adoleverint, exinde *titulos* quorundam, quibus nominibus nuncupentur, exinde *apparatus,* quibus superstitionibus instruantur, tum *loca,* quibus praesidibus dicentur, tum *artes,* quibus auctoribus deputentur." (*De Spect.* 4. 4)

[6] See the general treatments of Habel in *RE,* Suppl. v, cols. 608-630, *s.v.* "ludi publici"; Wissowa, *Religion und Kultus der Römer,* pp. 449-467; and André Piganiol, *Recherches sur les jeux romains.*

[7] "Honoris deum immortalium causa" (Livy vi. 42. 13); "ludi . . . facti sunt neque res ulla quae ad placandos deos pertineret praetermissa est" (Cic. *In Cat.* iii. 8. 20).

[8] See the list of *ludi* by Mommsen in *CIL,* I², pp. 299-301, and consult Albert Müller, "Das Bühnenwesen in der Zeit von Constantin der Grosse bis Justinian," *Neue Jahrbücher für das Klassische Altertum,* XXIII (1909), 36.

[9] See Jean Gagé, *Apollon romain,* pp. 400-407.

[10] See especially Piganiol, *Recherches sur les jeux romains,* passim.

[11] "The Temple above Pompey's Theater," *CJ,* XXXIX (1943-44), 360-365.

ants, although she concludes that the monument as conceived by Pompey and his architect was an aesthetic failure and was not afterwards copied.[12] The present study is in large part an expansion of her preliminary treatment, taking into account new archaeological material and carefully scrutinizing earlier material.[13]

[12] *Ibid.*, pp. 363-364: "A temple appearing on a hill above a great flight of steps is beautiful, but a temple high above a flight of steps with no natural foundation or reason for being there is ugly. . . . So Pompey's successors must have realized, and they never built another structure like it." This statement is hard to reconcile with her own brief mention (p. 361) of later examples of the combination.

[13] The only source cited by Hill for later *cavea* shrines is Wieseler, *Theatergebäude und Denkmäler des Bühnenwesens* (Göttingen, 1851).

CHAPTER I

THE SITES OF EARLY DRAMATIC PERFORMANCES

"In ipso Matris magnae conspectu . . ." (Cic. *Har. Resp.* 24)

THE SITES OF EARLY DRAMATIC
PERFORMANCES

AN INVESTIGATION of the combination of theater and temple in the fully developed
Roman theater building must begin with a search for precedents in the period
of the temporary theater. One must carefully establish what connection may
have existed in Rome between temples and the sites of dramatic performances previous
to the first stone theater in 55 B.C.

An attempt has already been made by Catharine Saunders to synthesize the available evidence for the sites of theatrical performances in Rome in the third and second
centuries B.C.[1] Miss Saunders defines the method to be used in deriving such information in the following terms:

> In the absence of direct evidence we may follow two main clues in the study of our
> problem. First, since dramatic performances in Republican times are regularly associated
> with *ludi*, we may ask where the various *ludi* were celebrated; and, secondly, in the recorded
> attempts to build theatres at Rome, we may seek to learn what principle, if any, determined
> the location of these theatres.[2]

However, it is not sufficient to know the official site of a given group of *ludi* in order
to derive the probable site of dramatic productions. On the other hand, there is a high
degree of probability that the various parts of a festival were regarded by the Romans
as distinct from one another, in significance as well as in time and place of presentation.
The following two passages, for example, strongly demand this interpretation: "Iam
ludi publici quoniam sunt cavea circoque divisi" (Cic. *Leg.* ii. 15. 38); "scaenicos
ludos per quadriduum, unum diem in circo fecit" (Livy xlii. 10.5).[3] One may also note
how carefully the various portions of the *ludi saeculares* are distinguished regarding
their sites in the official record.[4] Furthermore, although the days given to *ludi scaenici*
soon grew to outnumber those devoted to *ludi circenses* in all the major festivals, the

---

[1] "The Site of Dramatic Performances at Rome in the Times of Plautus and Terence," *TAPA*,
XLIV (1913), 87-97. This is the only place in which the subject has been dealt with as a whole,
previous and subsequent histories of the theater having handled it summarily.

[2] *Ibid.*, p. 88.

[3] Cf. Livy xxxiii. 25. 1; xl. 52. 3. In regard to the Cicero passage cited, Miss Saunders states,
"Here the contrast is not necessarily one of place; it is, conceivably, only a contrast in kinds of
entertainment." (*TAPA*, XLIV, 95) This view might be acceptable, if Cicero had used *scaena
circoque*, but *cavea* is never used in this sense, or any sense approaching it. (See *ThLL, s.v.*) She
further comments that the lateness of the passages, falling in a period when the construction of
"permanent" theaters has begun, destroys their value as evidence against the holding of *ludi
scaenici* in the circus. But Livy xxxiii. 25. 1 refers to 197 B.C., nearly twenty years before the first
recorded attempt to construct a theater. At any rate their value in this paper is not as negative
evidence—showing that scenic games were never presented in the circus—but rather as cautionary
signs, to prevent the positive assertion that if one category of *ludi* at a festival were held in the
circus, the others must also have been held there.

[4] Mommsen, *EphEp*, VIII, 268-272.

"name day" was always given over to circus games.[5] These retained their important position probably because of their greater force of tradition, dating from the days when they were the only form of *ludi* known to the Romans, before the importation of scenic games. Keeping all these facts in mind, one is forced to conclude that the appearance of the word *ludi* unqualified by an adjective descriptive of type, especially in the annalistic writing of Livy dealing with the third and second centuries, must never simply be assumed to refer to *ludi scaenici* without the support of further evidence.

The two oldest recorded Roman *ludi*, the Consualia and the Equirria, were both given at the altar of the god to whom the games were dedicated, the *ara Consi* in the valley between the Palatine and Aventine hills and the *ara Martis in campo*.[6] Both were festivals of the circus type and were never, as far as we know, associated with *ludi scaenici*. The two altars determined the sites of the two great circus buildings in Rome, the Circus Maximus and the Circus Flaminius.[7] That the Circus Maximus was under the tutelage of Consus was physically and permanently underlined by the presence of an underground sanctuary or *puteal* near one of the *metae*, which continued to be used throughout the history of the Circus.[8] It was uncovered on race days, apparently serving for all *ludi* celebrated there and not exclusively for the Consualia.[9]

A great deal of confusion surrounds the subject of the *ludi Romani*, confusion which is not the creation solely of modern scholars but exists in Livy's account, where the use of the terms *ludi Romani, ludi magni, ludi maximi, ludi votivi*, and simply *ludi* seems inextricably tangled. The standard view is Mommsen's, that the annual festival of the *ludi Romani* on the Ides of September developed from early irregular votive games, all of which were in honor of Iuppiter Optimus Maximus.[10] However, this view does not satisfactorily account for the occurrence again of special votive games during the late third and second centuries,[11] after the presumed regularization of the same type of *ludi* in 366. Nor does it account for the annalistic tradition that the great annual *ludi* date from the regal period and were founded by Tarquinius.

He waged war first with the Latins and captured one of their towns, Apiolae; . . . when the booty had been brought home he gave richer and more elaborate games than those of former kings. Then for the first time the site was designated as the circus, which is

---

[5] Or to the "epulum Iovis" in the *ludi Romani* and *Plebeii*. Wissowa, *Religion and Kultus der Römer*, p. 455.

[6] Habel in *RE*, Suppl. v, cols. 613-614, *s.v.* "ludi publici"; Wissowa, p. 450. When the Campus Martius was flooded, the Equirria were held in the "Campus Martialis" on the Caelian hill.

[7] Wissowa, p. 460.

[8] André Piganiol, *Recherches sur les jeux romains*, p. 1 and nn. 2-3.

[9] The expression of Plutarch (*Vit. Rom.* 14), cited by Piganiol (p. 1, n. 5), seems decisive: ἐν δὲ τοῖς ἱππικοῖς ἀγῶσιν.

[10] "Die ludi magni und Romani," *Röm. Forsch.*, ii, 42-57. This view is adopted by Wissowa, pp. 452-453; Saunders, *TAPA*, xliv, 89; Lily Ross Taylor, "The Opportunities for Dramatic Performances in the Time of Plautus and Terence," *TAPA*, lxviii (1937), 286; Habel in *RE*, Suppl. v, cols. 617-618.

[11] E.g., Livy xxvii. 33. 6; xxxi. 49. 4; xlii. 28. 8; and Suet. *Aug.* 23.

now called Maximus. . . . From that time there have been annually recurring games, variously known as "Romani" and "Magni."[12]

Both these circumstances are more satisfactorily explained, and the events of the year 366 become more comprehensible, under the theory advanced by Piganiol.[13] In his view the "creation" of the *ludi Romani* in 366 was actually an adoption by the state of an already established festival of the plebs; September games held in honor of Liber were usurped by Iuppiter Optimus Maximus and transformed into an official and city-wide ceremony. In the same year the plebeians were admitted to the consulship and the curule aedileship was created. The latter action was taken because, when the official nature of the *ludi* was changed and their scope increased, the plebeian aediles refused the additional liturgy, which was then assumed by patricians "honoris deum immortalium causa."[14] One of the main interests of this view is that it establishes for Roman dramatic festivals a certain connection, however tenuous, with Liber Pater, the official Roman counterpart to Dionysos, who is otherwise conspicuous in the history of the religious connections of the Roman stage by his absence.[15] It provides thus the only archaeological confirmation of Tertullian's statement: "Thus the theater of Venus is also the home of Liber. For they used to call other scenic games Liberalia, not only because they were vowed to Liber—these are the same as the Dionysia among the Greeks—but also because they were instituted by Liber."[16] This would absolve him from the accusation of simply analogizing from the history of the Greek theater. Of course the first official mention of *ludi scaenici* postdates the transformation of the games in 366. But the accepted date of these first scenic games, 364, is so close to that transformation that one strongly suspects that the introduction of *ludi scaenici*, despite Livy's statement that they were a "nova res bellicoso populo" (vii. 2. 3), was also an adoption of some feature of the September games of the plebs which, in terms of the later two-fold distinction of *ludi*, was more scenic than circensian.[17]

The Circus Maximus was the regular site of the *ludi circenses* belonging to this

[12] "Bellum primum cum Latinis gessit, et oppidum ibi Apiolas vi cepit; praedaque . . . revecta ludos opulentius instructiusque quam priores reges fecit. tunc primum circo, qui nunc maximus dicitur, designatus locus est . . . sollemnes deinde annui mansere ludi, Romani magnique varie appellati." (Livy i. 35. 7-10) Those who accept Mommsen's view punctuate with him: "sollemnes, deinde annui, mansere. . . ." This is a difficult reading of the Latin, which should rather mean: "from that time the games remained fixed at regular intervals, i.e., annual." "Annui" further explains "sollemnes," as in Livy iii. 15. 4: "ab Aequis statum iam ac prope sollemne in singulos annos bellum timebatur."

[13] *Recherches sur les jeux romains*, pp. 75-91, with a condensed statement on p. 91.

[14] Livy vi. 42. 13.

[15] See below, p. 17 and n. 45.

[16] "Itaque theatrum Veneris Liberi quoque domus est. Nam et alios ludos scaenicos Liberalia proprie vocabant, praeterquam Libero devotos, quae sunt Dionysia penes Graecos, etiam a Libero institutos." (*De Spect.* 10. 7)

[17] Livy does not even state definitely that the first *ludi scaenici* were given at the newly organized *ludi Romani*. The near coincidence in date, however, makes the assumption extremely probable, despite the doubts expressed by Saunders (*TAPA*, xliv, 89). The view that some forerunner of *ludi scaenici* may be found in an earlier Liberalia of the plebs has not, I think, been previously expressed.

1 1

festival, as well as of those belonging to the special *ludi votivi*, which seem to have paralleled the arrangements and time extension of the *ludi Romani* for any period.[18] There is no good evidence, however, for determining the site of the scenic games. The passage which seems most tempting at first, Livy's mention of the flood in the Circus which interrupted the *ludi* of 364 (vii. 3. 2), is open to precisely the same criticism as many other Livian mentions of *ludi*: we do not know to what portion of the festival reference is being made. In this instance, furthermore, the fact that Livy has been discussing the origins of *ludi scaenici* in the previous chapter does not remove the uncertainty. He describes the new form of *ludi* as being introduced only "inter alia caelestis irae placamina," and then, after a long digression on the origins of drama, picks up the recitation of events with the statement that the "placamina" did not work and the fears of the people were not alleviated, "cum medios forte ludos circus Tiberi superfuso irrigatus impedisset." Those who wish to use this statement as evidence for dramatic representations in the circus would have to interpret it as meaning that the *ludi scaenici*—which would in all likelihood have occupied only one day at this early period—had begun in the Circus Maximus in the morning when a sudden flood prevented their being continued. A more reasonable interpretation, however, would seem to be the following: Livy is using the word *ludi* to refer to a whole set of games covering several days, which, in accordance with the regular procedure, would consist of *ludi scaenici* followed by *ludi circenses*; in the midst of the games, then, while *ludi scaenici* were being presented at some other site, the Circus became so flooded as to prevent the continuation of the festival with *ludi circenses*. It is clear, then, that the conjecture in favor of the Circus Maximus as the site of the dramatic portions of the *ludi Romani* cannot stand for support on this passage from Livy, and no other independent evidence has been adduced for it. Other conjectures are even less firmly founded.[19]

That the *ludi Plebeii*, founded as a regular festival sometime before 216 B.C., were closely associated with the Circus Flaminius, constructed in the Campus Martius in 220, is unquestioned.[20] But that the dramatic presentations of that festival were given in the Circus Flaminius is certainly open to question in the absence of any evidence whatsoever to support this view.[21]

Similarly for the *ludi Apollinares*, no literary evidence associated with these

[18] Wissowa, p. 451; Taylor, *TAPA*, LXVIII, 296-297.

[19] Hahn, *Scaenicae Quaestiones Plautinae*, p. 4 (cited in Saunders, *TAPA*, XLIV, 94), conjectures "ad Capitolium," probably working on the principle of nearness to the temple of the festival deity, but offering no independent evidence. Michaut (*Sur les tréteaux latins*, p. 371) suggests the Forum as their site, supported by Saunders who considers it "not improbable" that the Forum was used for plays at the *ludi Romani*.

[20] Habel in *RE*, Suppl. V, cols. 620-621. Giuseppe Lugli, *I monumenti antichi di Roma e suburbio*, III, 15-16.

[21] Saunders maintains this, however, as "probable enough" (*TAPA*, XLIV, 90) and "very probable" (p. 94), although the only evidence she cites are two passages from Plautus, which she herself rightly proves "prove nothing" (p. 90, n. 23). See George E. Duckworth, *The Nature of Roman Comedy*, pp. 78-79.

games is sufficient to establish the site of their scenic presentations. Miss Saunders cites two passages from Livy with the implication that they strongly suggest the Circus Maximus as the site of the earliest presentations of dramas at this festival.[22] They do not. The first, "ludos praetor in circo maximo cum facturus esset" (Livy xxv. 12. 14), refers to the introduction of the festival in 212 B.C. In addition to the fact that Livy here is again using the unqualified *ludos*, it is not at all certain that *ludi scaenici* were even a part of the *Apollinares* at their founding.[23] The second passage, describing a flood which threatened to disturb the games in 202, can be shown in any case to refer specifically to *ludi circenses*:

> For the Tiber rose so high that the Circus was flooded and the *ludi Apollinares* were made ready outside the Porta Collina near the temple of Venus Erycina. But on the very day of the games a sudden clearing of the weather enabled the procession, which had set out toward the Porta Collina, to be recalled and led into the Circus.[24]

The expression *ludorum ipso die* ("on the very day of the games") can only refer to the thirteenth of July, which was the fixed date of the festival corresponding probably to the foundation date of the temple of Apollo, and which was devoted to *ludi circenses* even when the festival later became primarily a dramatic one.[25]

The *ludi Megalenses* during the second century provided more days for dramatic representations than any of the other regular festivals,[26] and it is in connection with these *ludi* that the most definite and secure literary evidence for the site of scenic games has come down to us. Cicero's oration *De haruspicum responso* contains a section (20-29) devoted to the pollution of the Megalensian games during the pontificate of Lentulus. The general importance of this section, in its revelation of the extent to which the purely religious side of *ludi scaenici* could be invoked even in the late Republic, can hardly be overemphasized.[27] Even more important for this study, however, is the specific information revealed in the following sentence: "For what shall I say about those games which our ancestors wished to be held on the Palatine, in front of the temple in the very sight of the Great Mother, at the Megalensian festival, games which are by tradition and rule extremely chaste, solemn, and religious?"[28]

[22] Saunders, *TAPA*, XLIV, 91.

[23] See Jean Gagé, *Apollon romain*, pp. 396-397. He cites the commemorative coin issues, which are restricted to representations of *ludi circenses*, and maintains, "Il est necessaire d'admettre que les premières célébrations avaient été essentiellement, peut-être exclusivement de cirque."

[24] "Nam ita abundavit Tiberis, ut ludi Apollinares circo inundato extra portam Collinam ad aedem Erucinae Veneris parati sint. ceterum ludorum ipso die subita serenitate orta pompa duci coepta ad portam Collinam revocata ductaque in circum est." (Livy xxx. 38. 11)

[25] Habel in *RE*, Suppl. v, col. 623.

[26] Perhaps six days, even from its establishment in 191. See Taylor, *TAPA*, LXVIII, 290.

[27] Of course one might maintain that this was only sophistry in Cicero's mouth, but nonetheless it would have to be sophistry consistent with the rational beliefs and emotional sympathies of his audience. An orator of Cicero's caliber would not take several pages to make a point regarded by the majority of his hearers as unfounded and irrelevant.

[28] "Nam quid ego de illis ludis loquar, quos in Palatio nostri maiores ante templum in ipso Matris magnae conspectu Megalesibus fieri celebrarique voluerunt, qui sunt more institutisque maxime casti, sollemnes, religiosi?" (*Har. Resp.* 24)

These games, then, were established to be held on the Palatine in front of the temple in the very sight of the goddess ("in ipso Matris magnae conspectu"). That *ludi scaenici* are specifically meant in this connection is apparent for two reasons. First, the whole section of the oration is dealing with a riotous incident which occurred during the scenic portion of the festival, as we know from the detail of the slaves being let onto the stage: "omne servitium permissu magistratus liberatum in alteram *scaenam* immissum, alteri praepositum." (25)[29] Second, the space left between the front of the temple of Magna Mater and the steep edge of the Palatine toward the Circus Maximus is certainly insufficient for the performance of *ludi circenses*.

Archaeological evidence can provide in this instance a quite specific picture of the physical relation between temple and performance site (Fig. 2).[30] The Palatine temple of Magna Mater stands on a high podium. Although some of the extant decoration dates from the Augustan reconstruction, the principal remains of the temple apparently predate this, going back at least to the reconstruction of Metellus in 111 B.C. It is likely that the form of the temple remained that of its original construction in 191. Below the front of the temple is a complex of walls of heavy masonry of various dates and functions, the interpretation of which presents many difficulties. It is in this sector of the Palatine that rock cuttings for prehistoric huts have been discovered in addition to monumental traces of walls and entrances to the Palatine from the early Republican period. Without the benefit of excavations, Hülsen nonetheless considered that the plays at the Megalensian games were presented in the open space in front of the temple, a space which he described as "klein und schmal . . . in der Kaiserzeit und nicht viel grösser in der republikanischen Epoche."[31] It is now possible to define that open space more adequately as a rather large rectangular area artificially built up to a level platform by means of a terrace wall (Fig. 2). Considerable portions of this wall are intact and can be regarded as contemporary with the original foundation of the temple.[32]

A hint as to the sense in which the games given on this terrace were literally "in ipso Matris magnae conspectu" is afforded by one of the reliefs, usually attributed to

[29] A perplexing question is incidentally raised by this passage, which seems to indicate the presence of two *scaenae*. The situation is unparalleled and extremely difficult either to explain or to explain away. Below there is a similar mention of two *caveae*: "tu in alteram servos immisisti, ex altera liberos eiecisti." (26) Were there two separate theaters in use at the same time, one on the platform beneath the temple and one below on the slope of the Palatine (see below, p. 25).

[30] The recent excavations of this area of the Palatine are not published. For the temple itself see the article of Hülsen, "Untersuchungen zur Topographie des Palatins: 1. Der Tempel der Magna Mater," *RM*, x (1895), 3-28; and the short notice in Lugli, *Roma antica, il centro monumentale*, pp. 431-434. Hülsen's conclusions are in the main validated by subsequent investigation. The description in this paragraph is based partly on a personal visit to the site together with Professor F. Castagnoli of the University of Rome.

[31] Hülsen, *RM*, x, 28.

[32] Although it is not possible to follow the complete line of this defining wall through the maze of earlier structures which it seems to cut across, and the recent excavations and investigations of the site have not been made available for detailed study through publication, this interpretation of the ruins has been accepted by Professor Romanelli, the director of these excavations.

the Ara Pietatis Augusti, now in the east façade of the Villa Medici (Fig. 3).[33] It is a representation of the front of a temple with a quite clear indication of the pediment sculptures.

In the angles are lionesses; next to them on either side are reclining male figures leaning on tambourines, one of which clearly holds a branch. In the center is a backless chair with a footstool; the chair is cushioned and draped with a cloth or veil falling to the left. On it is a mural crown with two towers and an opening or gate in front. The identity of the temple is clearly indicated not only by the lionesses, the reclining figures with tambourine and probably pine branch, who seem to be *archigalli,* and by the two corybantes which serve as acroteria. It is surely a temple of Magna Mater, and there seems no reason to doubt that it was the state temple on the Palatine.[34]

The chair in the center of the pediment is decked out as in a *sellisternium,* a rite which indeed has other connections with theatrical performances (See below, pp. 82-85). In such a rite the god's symbol or symbols represent the god himself seated on a specially prepared chair, to take part in a banquet or view a ceremony. In the present instance the turreted crown symbolizes the Great Mother herself, seated at the top of the front of her temple, in a position high above the crowd where she can watch the games being presented in her honor on the terrace below and be seen in turn by the participants in those games.[35]

Further support for the view that the goddess was in some real sense a spectator at these dramatic representations is given by two quotations from Christian writers. Arnobius, in discussing whether the gods in fact take pleasure in *ludi,* asks, "Is the Great Mother made calmer and more lenient by seeing the old story of Attis rehashed by actors?" Similarly, Augustine describes a certain spectacle as "that baseness which they act out in public in front of the mother of the gods, with a vast throng of both sexes watching and listening."[36] In view of the well-documented situation in front of the Palatine temple in Rome, there is no justification for refusing to accept a literal interpretation of these passages.

Furthermore, there is no inherent reason to regard the *ludi Megalenses* as essentially different from the other Roman cycles of *ludi.* In fact the government took care to "Romanize" this oriental cult and reduce its exotic elements as much as possible.[37]

---

[33] Reproduced in Lugli, *Roma antica, il centro monumentale,* p. 433. Described by M. Cagiano di Azevedo, *Le antichità di Villa Medici,* p. 14, with pl. IV; see also Inez Scott Ryberg, *Rites of the State Religion in Roman Art,* pp. 69-71, with pl. XXI bis, fig. 36c.

[34] I am indebted to Professor Lily Ross Taylor for permission to use her unpublished paper entitled "The Chair in the Pediment of the Palatine Temple of Magna Mater," delivered in Rome, May 1955. The above description is quoted from p. 2 of the typescript.

[35] "Le rituel veut que la divinité assiste aux jeux donnés en son honneur." (Henri Graillot, *Le culte de Cybèle Mère des Dieux à Rome et dans l'empire romain,* p. 86.)

[36] "Tranquillior, lenior Mater Magna efficitur, si Attidis conspexerit priscam refricari ab histrionibus fabulam?" (*Adv. Nat.* vii. 33)

"Illam . . . turpitudinem . . . quam per publicum agebant coram deum matre spectante atque audiente utriusque sexus frequentissima multitudine." (*De civ. D.* ii. 4)

[37] "Quant aux fêtes célébrées en son honneur par le peuple tout entier, les Megalensia, elles

Plautus' *Pseudolus* was presented at the dedication of the temple in 191 and possibly his *Trinummus* soon afterwards; Terence's *Andria, Hecyra, Heauton Timorumenos,* and *Eunuchus* were all performed before the Great Mother.[38] Later, it is true, there is evidence for the performance of legends based on the Cybele and Attis myth, stories which readily adapted themselves to the mime form and the taste of the later Roman audiences;[39] but mythological and religious travesty was a common subject for the Roman stage.

The temple of Flora on the slope of the Aventine hill was dedicated in 240 or 238 B.C., and appears to have been restored as late as the fourth century A.D. by the younger Symmachus.[40] The original dedication was celebrated by *ludi*, and the anniversary of this dedication, April 28, was marked by the regular *ludi Florales* after 173 B.C.[41] It seems reasonable to suppose that the mimes which formed the principal part of this festival were presented in front of the Aventine temple during the Republic, paralleling the *ludi Megalenses*, and evidence confirms such a situation for the late Empire. Augustine describes with rhetorical flourish the mimes held in Carthage in honor of Caelestis, whom he assimilates to the Roman Flora:

> Coming from every direction and standing wherever we could find room in front of the temple itself, where we used to see that statue placed, we would watch most intently the games that were going on. Glancing one way and then the other, we could see on this side the procession of prostitutes, and on that, the virgin goddess; she was most humbly adored, but in front of her, shameful acts were celebrated; we saw no modest mimes there, no bashful actress.[42]

A further reflection of this proximity of temple to stage is again found in Arnobius: "Does Flora think she is being honorably treated when she watches shameful deeds acted out during her festival and sees a procession from the houses of prostitution to the theaters?"[43]

The other regularly established festival during the Republic, the Cerialia or *ludi Ceriales,* offers no special evidence for the site of theatrical performances,[44] other than

---

n'avaient rien d'oriental mais furent organisées conformément aux traditions romaines." (Cumont, *Les religions orientales dans le paganisme romain*, p. 49.)

[38] Ritschl, *Parerga*, I, 292-296, 339-354; Taylor, *TAPA*, LXVIII, 290-291; Saunders, *TAPA*, XLIV, 91-92; Duckworth, p. 60.

[39] Reflected in the Arnobius quotation above. See Graillot, pp. 85-86, 141; and P. Charles Robert, "Les phases du mythe de Cybèle et d'Atys rappelées par les médaillons contorniates," *RN*, Ser. III, Vol. III (1885), 32-48.

[40] Platner-Ashby, *A Topographical Dictionary of Ancient Rome*, p. 209, s.v. "Flora, aedes."

[41] Taylor, *TAPA*, LXVIII, 291; Habel in *RE*, Suppl. V, col. 625.

[42] "Ante ipsum tamen delubrum, ubi simulacrum illud locatum conspiciebamus, universi undique confluentes et ubi quisque poterat stantes ludos qui agebantur intentissimi spectabamus, intuentes alternante conspectu hinc meretriciam pompam, illinc virginem deam: illam suppliciter adorari, ante illam turpia celebrari; non ibi pudibundos mimos, nullam verecundiorem scaenicam vidimus." (*De civ. D.* ii. 26)

[43] "Existimatve tractari se honorifice Flora, si suis in ludis flagitiosas conspexerit res agi, et migratum ab lupanaribus in theatra?" (*Adv. Nat.* vii. 33)

[44] They are not mentioned in Saunders (*TAPA*, XLIV, 87-97), although Taylor (*TAPA*, LXVIII,

what might be assumed from the location of the temple of its tutelary divinity. The temple of Ceres, Liber and Libera, known to the Romans mainly by the shortened title "aedes Cereris,"[45] is situated on the slope of the Aventine overlooking the western end of the Circus Maximus.[46] Its topographical relationship with the Circus was in fact so close that the site of the temple could actually be described as ἐπὶ τοῖς τέρμασι τοῦ μεγίστου τῶν ἱπποδρόμων ὑπὲρ αὐτὰς ἰδρυμένος τὰς ἀφέσεις.[47] The circensian games of this festival, then, were literally given under the eyes of the goddess who was honored,[48] with a topographical relationship paralleling that of the *ludi Florales* and *ludi Megalenses*. It is impossible to state definitely that the *ludi scaenici*, which occupied seven days of the festival during the Empire, were also presented in the Circus Maximus, but it is in this festival, rather than in the case of the *ludi Romani* and *Plebeii*, that the supposition of scenic games in the circus might most justifiably be made.

In addition to the regularly recurring festival cycles and votive games to Iuppiter Optimus Maximus, *ludi scaenici* were also presented as part of funeral celebrations and at the dedications of temples. Although no direct and incontrovertible evidence can be brought to bear on the site of the dramatic performances which could be a part of *ludi funebres*, Saunders is probably to be followed in assigning them to the Forum Romanum, at least as a possible, though not an exclusive, location.[49] There is no religious connection apparent in the site itself.[50]

We know that the dedication of a temple was frequently accompanied by *ludi*, and that these could include *ludi scaenici*.[51] It is never specifically stated where these

---

289) gives them at least two days of *ludi scaenici* during the second century. In general see Habel in *RE*, Suppl. v, cols. 624-625; Wissowa, pp. 299-302.

[45] Cicero (*Verr.* v. 14. 36) says, "mihi ludos sanctissimos . . . Cereri Libero Liberaeque faciundos." Otherwise, the Romans apparently seldom expressed the relationship of Liber to these games. The aetiological connection, if real, hardly impressed itself on the minds of the Romans. (See above, p. 11.)

[46] Platner-Ashby, pp. 109-110, *s.v.* "Ceres Liber Liberaque, aedes."

[47] ". . . at the end of the Circus Maximus, erected directly above the starting gates." (Dion. Hal. *Ant. Rom.* vi. 94. 3)

[48] Also under the eyes of her priest. See Piganiol, *Recherches sur les jeux romains*, pp. 85-86: "La place du magistrat présidant les jeux est précisément au-dessus des *carceres*: en d'autres termes, le président des jeux du grand cirque est, à l'origine, identique au prêtre ou au gardien du temple de Cérès, Liber et Libera."

[49] Saunders, *TAPA*, xliv, 93-94. The most conclusive evidence is given by Livy xxxi. 50. 4: "Et ludi funebres eo anno per quadriduum in foro mortis causa M. Valeri Laevini a Publio et Marco filiis eius facti, et munus gladiatorium datum ab iis; paria quinque et viginti pugnarunt." Here, and only here, there seems no doubt that the *ludi* and not just the *munera* were given "in foro," from the order of Livy's statement. Saunders is mistaken in stating that "*ludi funebres* included both circensian and scenic features," since our evidence only suggests *munera* and *ludi scaenici*. Cf. Taylor, *TAPA*, lxviii, 299. The second prologue of the *Hecyra* (vv. 39-42) is not as conclusive as Hahn (*Scaenicae Quaestiones Plautinae*, p. 3; cited by Saunders, p. 93) and Saunders indicate. At most it reveals that the gladiatorial shows and plays were given at sites near one another, and we cannot be certain of the site of these particular *munera*.

[50] But for the religious significance possible through the *pompa*, see below, p. 86.

[51] Temple of Juventas in 191: Livy xxxvi. 36. 7; temples of Juno Regina and Diana in 179: Livy xl. 52. 1-3; temple of Fortuna Equestris in 173: Livy xlii. 10. 5. The custom was still referred

ludi scaenici were performed. In such cases, however, it seems almost certain that the performances occurred in the vicinity of the temple involved. If not in front of the temple, they would at least be presented within sight of it, the precise location being determined by the nature of the ground and the available open space. This supposition seems valid for two reasons, the one inherent in the situation itself, which would logically call for a close topographical relation between the ceremony and its focal point, just as we should today expect the ceremonies for the dedication of a post office to be held on the post office steps and not in a stadium several miles away. The second reason is drawn from a consideration of the *ludi Florales* and *Megalenses*, both of which grew out of temple dedications and were celebrated on their anniversaries, and both of which had established theatrical sites, as we have shown above, in front of the pertinent temple. It is logical to assume that the dedication *ludi* for both the temple of Flora and that of Magna Mater were given on essentially the same sites as the later recurrent *ludi* and thence suggest sites of a similar nature for other sporadic temple dedication games which did not grow into regular festival cycles.

The second category of evidence available in investigating the early sites of Roman dramatic performances is the literary record of the construction of theaters. Three such structures are specifically alluded to in Livy.

The earliest, and most important for this study, is the "theatrum et proscaenium ad Apollinis," for which the censors of the year 179 B.C. let a contract.[52] There has been considerable disagreement among scholars on the question of the "permanence" of this theater, and it has even been maintained that the contract was never actually carried out.[53] Its duration, however, is of no immediate concern to the problem here treated. The value of the passage is rather that it provides absolute assurance of the construction, or at least a plan for the construction, of a stage and an auditorium "near the temple of Apollo." To specify this location requires an attempt to clarify a recent controversy over the question of the number of temples of Apollo in Rome during the Republic. Asconius, commenting on a topographical reference in Cicero's *In Toga Candida*, makes the following statement:

> This passage is entirely clear. But so that you do not make a mistake, thinking that the temple of Apollo on the Palatine was the noblest at this time, you must be advised that this temple is not the one that Cicero means, since Caesar—later called the Divine Augustus —built it many years after the death of Cicero, after the victory at Actium. He wishes, rather, to indicate the temple which is outside the Porta Carmentalis between the Forum Holitorium and the Circus Flaminius. For that was the only temple of Apollo in Rome at the time.[54]

---

to by Lactantius (*Div. Inst.* vi. 20. 34): "nam ludorum celebrationes deorum festa sunt, si quidem ob natales eorum vel templorum novorum dedicationes sunt constituti." *Ludi scaenici* were also held at the dedication of statues of divinities. (See, e.g., *CIL*, VIII, 858, 7984.)

[52] Livy xl. 51. 3.

[53] Fabia, "Les théâtres de Rome," *RevPhil*, XXI (1897), 16-17.

[54] "Omnia sunt manifesta. Ne tamen erretis, quod his temporibus aedes Apollinis in Palatio fuit nobilissima, admonendi estis non hanc a Cicerone significari, utpote quam post mortem etiam

Such a clear and definite assertion by an otherwise trustworthy commentator living in the first half of the first century A.D. would seem to need no defense, but it has been violently, and copiously, called into question by some twentieth century archaeologists.[55] In their view, a second temple of Apollo existed during the Republic, which grew out of an Italic temple of Veiovis, resulting in a sort of combined Veiovis-Apollo cult center. A basis for their arguments does exist in an inconsistency in Livy, who, after recording under the year 431 the dedication of the temple of Apollo vowed "pro valetudine populi" in 433, has another entry referring to the dedication of the (or "a") temple of Apollo in 353.[56] Since the same temple would not be dedicated, in the normal sense of the word, twice, Livy seems here to give evidence for the existence of two temples of Apollo in Rome. These two passages, then, will not stand together with the statement of Asconius without some explanation which will resolve their apparent inconsistency. The whole controversy over the number of temples of Apollo in Rome, cluttered as it has become with "supporting" evidence, can be reduced essentially to the following question: which of the two passages—the second Livy entry or the statement of Asconius—can be most successfully defended in a literal sense; or, stating the question more fruitfully, which of the passages can most logically be re-interpreted in such a manner as to remove the inconsistency?

Livy's statement is completely bare of detail. The mention of the dedication of the temple comes as an appendix to a sentence describing the end of a year of cam-paigning in Faliscan territory.[57] Not only is no detail of the cause, person, place, or

---

Ciceronis multis annis Imp. Caesar, quem nunc Divum Augustum dicimus, post Actiacam victoriam fecerit; sed illam demonstrari quae est extra portam Carmentalem inter forum Holitorium et circum Flaminium. ea enim sola tum quidem Romae Apollinis aedes." (p. 90, ed. Clark, *OCT*)

[55] Luigi Du Jardin, "Monumenti antichi dell'area di S. Nicola ai Cesarini," *RendPontAcc*, Ser. III, Vol. VIII (1931-32), 29-151. This long article is devoted almost entirely to the establishment of the two-Apollo theory, which was taken up in slightly different form and most passionately defended by Giuseppe Marchetti-Longhi. It finds its way into most of his articles (for which see the Bibliography) but is most fully treated in "Il culto ed i tempii di Apollo in Roma prima di Augusto," *RM*, LVIII (1943), 27-47. He has received outspoken opposition at the hands of Giuseppe Lugli. See especially "L'origine dei teatri stabili in Roma antica secondo i recenti studi," *Dioniso*, IX (1942), 55-64. A better, dispassionate, critique of some of the arguments adduced by the dual-ists may be found in F. Castagnoli, "Note di topografia romana," *BullComm*, LXXIV (1951-52), 53-55. Although there are certain differences between Du Jardin's and Marchetti-Longhi's views, and it is often impossible for the reader to know which of the two cults is meant at any given time in the latter's exposition, I have tried in what follows to present the clearest possible state-ment of the theory in its minimum essential form.

[56] "Pestilentia eo anno aliarum rerum otium praebuit. aedis Apollini pro valetudini populi vota est." (Livy iv. 25. 3)

"Cn. Iulius consul aedem Apollinis absente collega sine sorte dedicavit. aegre id passus Quinctius cum dimisso exercitu in urbem redisset, nequiquam in senatu est conquestus." (Livy iv. 29. 7)

"In Faliscos eodem noxios crimine vis belli conversa est, sed hostes nusquam inventi. cum populatione peragrati fines essent, ab oppugnatione urbium temperatum; legionibusque Romam reductis reliquum anni muris turribusque reficiendis consumptum, et aedis Apollinis dedicata est." (Livy vii. 20. 9)

[57] Livy vii. 20. 9. Text cited above, n. 56.

ceremony connected with the dedication mentioned, but also there is no previous reference to the vowing of the temple or explanation of the circumstances leading to its construction, contrary to Livy's usual practice. This in itself is sufficient to render the passage suspect, if not as to text, at least as to interpretation. The simplest re-interpretation is that the sentence refers actually to a rededication of the fifth century temple of Apollo after some reconstruction which either Livy or his source failed to mention.[58] Such a failure is more readily understandable than would be complete silence on the circumstances of the dedication of a new temple. Those who adopt the two-temple view, however, must not only rest satisfied with this silence but must also maintain that Livy is here manifesting an error, in which he is according to them not alone, in confusing Veiovis and Apollo and projecting that confusion back into the fourth or fifth century. Furthermore, they must then maintain that Asconius makes the opposite error: that he, alone of all our sources, is aware that the temple of the "Italic Apollo" is more properly to be called a temple of Veiovis, and therefore, as a point of erudition, there was only one genuine temple of Apollo in Rome before Augustus.[59] But they wish to retain as referring to the temple of "Veiovis-Apollo" a great number of the occurrences of "aedes Apollinis" in Livy and elsewhere—including the "theatrum et proscaenium ad Apollinis" of 179 B.C.—and have not countered with a single instance of the use of "aedes Veiovis" to refer to this temple.[60] It is hardly necessary to emphasize the highly subjective nature of such hypotheses.

If in addition, however, archaeological evidence were found which established with a high degree of probability the existence of a second temple of Apollo, the state-ment of Asconius would be outweighed. Marchetti-Longhi and Du Jardin have tried to show that this temple has actually been excavated, and is to be identified with

[58] "Si le texte de Tite-Live est exact—et toute hypothèse de corruption est exclue,—et s'il s'applique au même temple, il faut admettre, soit que l'historien a omis de placer plus haut dans son récit un détail explicatif (par exemple, la mention d'un dommage accidentel), soit qu'une nouvelle dédicace fut rendue nécessaire au milieu du IVᵉ siècle par un épisode ultérieur au sac gaulois, ou encore par un accident de nature surtout religieuse." (Gagé, *Apollon romain*, pp. 102-103)

[59] Du Jardin denies the validity of the confusion with Veiovis as a motivating force in explain-ing our textual inconsistencies, but is in turn driven into an impossible display of sophistry in justifying the statement of Asconius. This will be seen from a partial quotation of his argument: "Volle, insomma, Asconio avvertire come, nella sua semplicità, l'espressione *aedes Apollinis*, adoprata da Cicerone, non avrebbe potuto ingenerare in chi leggesse errore, dacchè con essa, quando l'oratore scriveva, cioè prima dell'edificazione del tempio di Apollo Palatino, non s'usava designare se non il vetustiore sacrario del nume. Al che deducesi conferma dal fatto che il secondo tempio di Apollo dei prati Flamini all'epoca di Cicerone appellavasi, vedemmo, *aedes Apollinis Medici*, mentre nell'età d'Asconio era chiamato *delubrum* o *templum Apollinis Sosiani*; dal che desumesi d'altronde, sempre all'epoca d'Asconio . . . , essersi diffusa nell'Urbe la consuetudine di nominare abbreviatamente: *aedes Apollinis*, pur il santuario del Palatino." (Du Jardin, *Rend PontAcc*, Ser. III, Vol. VIII, 81-82.)

[60] Livy elsewhere correctly refers to Veiovis, if we accept the nearly certain emendation of xxxv. 41. 8: "aedes duae Iovi eo anno in Capitolio dedicatae sunt" ("duae Iovi"="Veiovi" or "Vediovi"). See the discussion in Gagé, *Apollon romain*, pp. 104-106.

Temple C of the Largo Argentina area.[61] Three pieces of evidence have been adduced to support this identification; one appears to be a completely false interpretation, and the other two are utterly inconclusive. The first is a large cult statue found between Temples B and C which Du Jardin attempts to attribute to Apollo in spite of its obviously feminine characteristics.[62] This attribution has found no acceptance among other scholars and is denied even by Marchetti-Longhi, who associates the statue with Temple B.[63] The second is the use by Vitruvius (iii. 3. 4) of "Apollinis et Dianae aedes" as an example of a diastyle temple: the "Sosianus" temple is not diastyle, while Temple C of the Largo Argentina group is. However, the coupling of Diana with Apollo does not fit either the "Sosianus" temple or the supposed second temple to an "Italic Apollo,"[64] but is more appropriate to the Augustan temple on the Palatine.[65] Furthermore this temple, important to Augustan religious policy, was dedicated in 28 B.C., very near the probable date of composition of Vitruvius' work, and is therefore almost certainly the building referred to in the Vitruvius passage.[66] The third piece of evidence used by Marchetti-Longhi is an inscription dedicated to Apollo by a certain "parasitus Apollinis"—an actor or other theatrical employee—and found in the Largo Argentina excavations.[67] Especially since it was not found in a position which definitely connects it with Temple C, the presence of such a votive inscription in the approximate vicinity does not add enough force to the proposed identification to counterbalance the insufficiency of the other evidence adduced.[68]

It must be concluded, then, that although Marchetti-Longhi wishes to associate

---

[61] Du Jardin, *RendPontAcc*, Ser. iii, Vol. viii, 84-133; Marchetti-Longhi, *RM*, lviii, 42-46. The first publication of the temple is by Marchetti-Longhi in *BullComm*, lx (1932), 253-346. The problem of identifying the divinities of these temples is vexed. See the bibliography in Lugli, *Monumenti antichi di Roma e suburbio*, iii, 26, and the summary, *ibid.* pp. 49-50 and 66-70. The most recent treatment of the area is by Castagnoli ("Il Campo Marzio nell'antichità," *MemLinc*, Ser. viii, Vol. i [1947], 169-175). Steering clear of swampy religious assumptions, the author, first by a careful process of elimination and then by the addition of the positive support of archaeologically sound dating from stratification and some evidence from sculpture finds, proposes the following identifications: A, Iuno Curritis, middle of the third century B.C.; B, Fortuna Huiusce Diei, 100 B.C.; C, Feronia, beginning of the third century B.C.

[62] Du Jardin, *RendPontAcc*, Ser. iii, Vol. viii, 100-113, 147-151.

[63] "Apollinar, Senatus ad Apollinis e Curia Pompeiia," *RendPontAcc*, Ser. iii, Vol. xx (1943-44), p. 434 and n. 103.

[64] Gagé, *Apollon romain*, p. 162.

[65] *Ibid.*, pp. 527-528. But for another explanation see Castagnoli, *BullComm*, lxxiv, 54.

[66] The Palatine shrine has now been identified with near certainty as the temple, once attributed to Iuppiter Victor, immediately west of the *domus Flavia*. See Gagé, *Apollon romain*, pp. 555-569.

[67] Text in Giuseppe Marchetti-Longhi, "Gli scavi del Largo Argentina," *BullComm*, lxxi (1943-45), 80, correcting an earlier reading in *RM*, lviii, 27: Deo Sancto Apollini/M (arcus) Plaetorius M (arci) l (ibertus) Nicon/parasitus Apollinis et/q (uin)q (uennalis) collegi cantorum/ d (ono) d (edit).

[68] It was found "nello sterro del tempio rotondo [B] fra questo ed il prossimo tempio C." Marchetti-Longhi himself says, "Un tal complesso di carattere teatrale in un cippo rinvenuto in questo luogo, proprio al confine del gruppo del Teatro di Pompeo, non sorprende certamente." (*BullComm*, lxxi, 80-81.) Cf. A. Degrassi in *Doxa*, ii (1949), 63.

the "theatrum et proscaenium ad Apollinis" of 179 B.C. with one of the Republican temples of the Largo Argentina area, and thence to proceed to equate its site with that of the later theater of Pompey (see below, p. 49), it must rather be associated with the known "Sosianus" temple of Apollo and considered in conjunction with the later theater of Marcellus.

The value of this conclusion is apparent when we consider that the pattern of this conjunction is physically visible today, through the virtual rebuilding of both theater and temple during the Augustan period (Fig. 1). C. Sosius, an Antonian who was consul in 32 B.C., undertook to rebuild the temple of Apollo after his triumph "ex Judaea" in 34, perhaps as a countermove against Augustus' already apparent religious policy in favor of Apollo.[69] The reconstruction was complete for the superstructure but, as recent excavations have demonstrated, Sosius respected the site and essential plan of the original Republican temple, which was hexastyle and rested on a high podium.[70] Only at the front was it necessary to modify the original plan by somewhat shortening the *pronaos* and moving the entrance steps to the sides, after Augustus resumed the construction of the theater of Marcellus. The original plan for the theater was Caesar's, who had demolished the temple of Pietas and purchased certain private property in the area to make room for it.[71] The project, however, seems to have been abandoned upon his death, perhaps because of lack of popular sympathy, and was not taken up until several years later by Augustus, who embraced it with wholehearted sympathy and dedicated the finished structure in the name of his nephew Marcellus in 13 or 11 B.C.[72]

It is inconceivable that the site of this theater "ad Apollinis" was regarded as either insignificant or accidental. The façade of the temple nearly touches the circumference of the *cavea* at a point near the central axis. Although not elevated to a point where it could be seen over the auditorium from the inside of the theater, it nonetheless stands on a high podium, which was apparently raised in the Sosian reconstruction,[73] and would suggest from the outside a sort of parallel to the theater of Pompey and temple of Venus Victrix (Fig. 18), which Caesar certainly would have been trying to rival when he formed his project.[74] Augustus in the *Res Gestae* defines the location of the theater as "ad aedem Apollinis,"[75] and the reverse phenomenon, the specification of the temple of Apollo by the phrase "ad theatrum Marcelli," seems

[69] Gagé, *Apollon romain*, pp. 494-496.

[70] On these excavations see A. M. Colini, "Il tempio di Apollo," *BullComm*, LXVIII (1940), 9-40, and pls. I-IV; Fuhrmann in *AA*, LVI (1941), cols. 508-516.

[71] Pliny *HN* vii. 121; Cass. Dio xliii. 49. 3.

[72] Cass. Dio liv. 26. 1; *Mon. Anc.* iv. 22. That the project had not been carried far, or perhaps had been entirely abandoned, is apparent from the fact that Augustus also had to purchase land in order to complete the construction.

[73] It stood 5.7 meters above the foundation. See Fuhrmann in *AA*, LVI (1941), col. 511.

[74] See below, Chapter III. The aspect of conscious rivalry, in addition to the fact that it is deducible from the situation itself, is expressed by Cass. Dio (xliii. 49. 3): θέατρόν τέ τι κατὰ τὸν Πομπήιον οἰκοδομῆσαι ἐθελήσας προκατεβάλετο μὲν, οὐκ ἐξετέλεσε δέ.

[75] *Mon. Anc.* iv. 22. In Greek, πρὸς τῷ Ἀπόλλωνος ναῷ.

to have been standard, having come down to us in the *fasti*.[76] Although the theater was not yet dedicated in 17 B.C., it was used for a portion of the *ludi saeculares*,[77] which formed a part of the Apollonian propaganda of Augustus. Jean Gagé has maintained that the construction of the theater of Marcellus was consciously used by Augustus to absorb the "Sosian" Apollo into his personal-political cultivation of the god, in the same way that he used the "coincidence" of his birthday with that of the "Sosian" temple.[78] It seems extremely likely, then, that an ideological as well as topographical relation exists between the theater of Marcellus and the temple of Apollo Sosianus, nor does it seem possible that such a union is merely coincidentally suggested for the period a century and a half earlier by the phrase "theatrum et proscaenium ad Apollinis." Lugli, in his map of the theater area of Rome, places the "temporary" theater of 179 B.C. immediately in front of and on the axis of the temple, with the façade of the temple facing the rear of the *cavea*.[79] With a low auditorium wall, the god could be a spectator at the theatrical games in the precise sense which was defined above for the temple of Magna Mater on the Palatine. This corresponds almost exactly with the position of the later theater of Marcellus, except that the latter is slightly off center with regard to the temple.[80] This view has been criticized on the grounds that there would not have been enough space in front of the temple for a temporary theater if, as our sources indicate, the temple of Pietas had to be removed, the temple of Apollo had to be shortened, and private houses bought and demolished to permit the construction of the theater of Marcellus.[81] Neither the temple of Pietas, which had been built before 179 B.C.,[82] nor the additional few feet on the temple of Apollo confined the available space enough to prevent the setting up of a "theatrum et proscaenium," as long as it was but slightly smaller than the present "theatrum Marcelli," and it would be strange if it were not smaller at such an early period. The large number of private houses demolished, however, does seem to prove that there was no theater existing on the spot, or free space to accommodate a temporary theater at regular intervals, at the time at which Caesar formed the project for his new theater. But it does not prove that such was the case in 179 B.C., or even that such was the case twenty years previous to Caesar's plan, since houses were being built and crowded into every available corner of land with great rapidity as the population of the city grew.

[76] *CIL*, I², pp. 215, 252.

[77] *CIL*, VI, 32323. 157; comment in Mommsen, *EphEp*, VIII, p. 271.

[78] Gagé, *Apollon romain*, pp. 398, 497-498.

[79] *Dioniso*, IX, tav. I, opp. p. 56.

[80] An additional argument for the hypothesis of the identity of the sites seems to me to lie in the fact that the theater of Marcellus is oriented in such a way that the river prevents the construction of a full-fledged *porticus post scaenam* in accordance with the precept of Vitruvius and the example of Pompey's theater. This is perhaps best explained in terms of a desire to respect the orientation of an earlier "theatrum et proscaenium ad Apollinis," so that the temple would lie at the *back* of the *cavea* near its midpoint.

[81] Giuseppe Marchetti-Longhi, " 'Theatrum Marcelli' e 'Mons Fabiorum,' " *RendPontAcc*, Ser. III, Vol. XX (1943-44), 95-96.

[82] It was dedicated in 181 B.C. See Platner-Ashby, p. 390, *s.v.* "Pietas, aedes."

It cannot be ascertained how long the original (if it was in fact the original)[83] "theatrum et proscaenium ad Apollinis" lasted, beyond the fact that it probably was not still in existence in 154 B.C. when the censors stopped the construction of a stone theater and decreed against the use of seats at public spectacles.[84] Nor can it be ascertained whether or not there was a continuous tradition of temporary theaters at this site, beyond the fact that there was probably no such arrangement in the years immediately preceding 45 B.C. What is certain is that there are two documented instances in Rome of a theater "ad Apollinis." In the light of our otherwise scanty evidence this fact strongly suggests a tradition, though interrupted, of the presentation of *ludi scaenici* in front of the temple of Apollo in such a way that they were "in conspectu dei."

The second theatrical construction reflected in our sources is the "scaenam aedilibus praetoribusque praebendam," contracted for by the censors of 174 B.C., but it furnishes no evidence regarding sites.[85]

A third instance of the construction, or the attempt to construct, a theater is recorded for the censors of 155 B.C., but the theater was destroyed at its inception by P. Cornelius Scipio Nasica, in conjunction with the decree prohibiting the use of seats for spectators at games.[86] Its location is mentioned by Velleius Paterculus (i. 15. 3): "Cassius censor a Lupercali in Palatium versus theatrum facere instituit." The exact interpretation of this passage is not clear. The Lupercal was a sacred area at the bottom of the slope at the southwest corner of the Palatine, approximately under the temple of Magna Mater.[87] It lies, if one speaks in terms of the early topographical division of the hill, on the Germalus rather than on the Palatium. F. W. Shipley's rendering of the Velleius passage, "a theatre beginning at the Lupercal and facing the Palatine,"[88] is unacceptable, for it makes Cassius' theater face uphill, either directly or obliquely, depending on whether we take "Palatium" to refer to the whole hill or its eastern peak. This is entirely unfeasible, and the passage must rather be taken to describe the position, and not the orientation, of the structure. Thus it should be translated, "a theater located in the direction of the Palatine from the Lupercal," or "on the Palatine side of the Lupercal." This would most likely signify an area on the slope of the Germalus near the saddle, probably in the vicinity of the later temple of

---

[83] One need hardly emphasize the accidental quality of our evidence. Livy says nothing about this being the first.

[84] Livy *Epit.* xlviii; Val. Max. ii. 4. 2.

[85] Livy xli. 27. 5. The inference drawn by Saunders (*TAPA*, XLIV, 92) is gratuitous: "We do not know its site, but the fact that it was to be available for *ludi* under the care of all these officials—the *ludi Romani, plebei, Megalenses, Apollinares*—shows that proximity to the shrine of the god of the *ludi* was not an absolute requirement, at any rate in 174 B.C." The mention of praetors can tell us nothing about what festivals were intended to be performed at this theater, since, with the exception of a single instance for the *ludi Apollinares* of 211 B.C., praetors were never entrusted with the *cura ludorum*. See Mommsen, *Römisches Staatsrecht*, II¹ 517-522.

[86] See above, n. 84.

[87] Its boundaries are not clear, although its general location is well established. See Lugli, *Roma antica, il centro monumentale*, pp. 420-423.

[88] Velleius Paterculus, *Compendium of Roman History*, "Loeb Classical Library," London, 1924.

Apollo. The attempt of Ribbeck to associate this theater with the temple of Magna Mater and thus with the *ludi Megalenses* is possibly correct.[89] In other words, Cassius may have been attempting to construct a regular *theatrum* in a position below the terrace on which the Megalensian games were regularly held but still near enough to replace that terrace as a site "in ipso Matris magnae conspectu." But the evidence is not strong enough, nor the text of Velleius sure enough, to make this more than a possible hypothesis. On the other hand there is no evidence to support Marchetti-Longhi's attempt to connect this theater with the chthonic, swamp-dwelling divinities of the Velabrum,[90] which lies outside the area allowed by the text of Velleius.

A tabulation of the results of this detailed enquiry into the sites of *ludi scaenici* yields the following picture:

Ludi Romani	?
Ludi Plebeii	?
Ludi Apollinares	?
Ludi Megalenses	"ante templum in ipso Matris magnae conspectu"
Ludi Florales	"ante ipsum delubrum"
Ludi Ceriales	in Circo Maximo = ante ipsum delubrum (?)
Ludi funebres	in Foro
Ludi pro dedicatione templi	ante ipsum delubrum (?)
Theatrum—179 B.C.	"ad Apollinis" (ante aedem)
Theatrum—174 B.C.	?
Theatrum—155 B.C.	"in Palatium versus" (ante templum Matris magnae?)

With the exception of *ludi funebres*—which were not dedicated to a "divinity" of the same type as the others—all sites for *ludi scaenici* which can be located with certainty or probability before the erection of a permanent theater in Rome are not only connected with a temple but are further specified as in front of a temple. Whether or not this was restricted to the particular god honored in the festival depends on the interpretation placed on the construction of the short-lived theaters during the first half of the second century, whether or not they were meant to be used exclusively for one festival cycle. There is no real evidence to suggest that they were not.[91] However, one would reasonably infer that if they were actually permanent and monumental, economy would demand that they be used more frequently than during one festival each year. Nonetheless the practice can be seen to have differed in respect to site from that followed with the *ludi circenses*, for which the choice of a site was, of course, also restricted by the nature of the games. The latter were given, as far as we know, in only two places, the Circus Maximus and the Circus Flaminius. Here the religious

---

[89] *Römische Tragödie*, p. 649, n. 11; cited and apparently accepted by Saunders, *TAPA*, XLIV, 92.

[90] "Indubbiamente il luogo fu scelto proprio in rapporto ai culti ed alle divinità infere del paludoso Velabro, che erano del tutto analoghi a quelli del Campo, onde, in tal guisa, l'eccezione conferma la regola [that all theaters were associated with divinities worshiped in the swampy area of the Campus Martius!]" ("Religione e teatro, l'influenza religiosa nella topografia dei teatri di Roma antica," *Dioniso*, IX [1942], 10.)

[91] See above, n. 85.

connections insofar as they depend upon the *loca* are fixed, apparently connected rather with the origins of the type of *ludi* than with the eponymous god being honored by the particular *ludi*.[92]

[92] See above, p. 10. In addition to Consus (for which see Piganiol, pp. 1-14) many other divinities were represented by shrines and altars along the *spina*. (See Lugli, *Roma antica, il centro monumentale*, p. 604.) Our knowledge of the Circus Flaminius is much less secure, but it probably contained many analogous physical representations of divinities. See Marchetti-Longhi, "Il Circo Flaminio," *MemLinc*, Ser. v, Vol. xvi (1922), 621-770; and, more briefly, Lugli, *I monumenti antichi*, iii, 14-23.

CHAPTER II
THE ARCHITECTURAL PATTERN

"Cui subiecimus . . . gradus spectaculorum" (Tert. *De Spect.* 10. 5)

THE ARCHITECTURAL PATTERN

THE EXISTENCE of a tradition of dramatic performances in front of temples, "in conspectu dei," may be called the "ideological" pattern for Pompey's theater. It remains to be determined, however, what models in a more strictly physical sense may have existed previous to Pompey's theater to suggest the architectural pattern for combining temple with theatrical *cavea* and stage.

The logical starting point for such a search is Greece, since Greek drama is intimately connected by its origins with religion, and retained close associations, at least in the Athenian sphere, with the worship of Bacchus. It is striking, under these conditions, that not a single known Greek theater is architecturally bound to a temple and further that topographical connections between the two, when they exist, are loose, unstressed, unsystematic.

The closest visible relation with a temple among Greek theaters was at Athens itself, where the orchestra was placed within the precinct of Dionysos beside the older temple, but in such a way that there was a road between the two during the earliest period, and the stage building completely hid the temple in the later periods (Fig. 4).[1] At Delphi the theater is also within the sacred precinct, on the level above the main temple of Apollo, and the theaters are located near, though not within, sanctuaries at Delos, Epidauros, Cyrene, and Syracuse.[2] In not a single instance, however, has any attempt been made to join theater and temple as a single organism.

Pompey himself, according to Tertullian, spoke of his theater as "a temple under which we have placed steps for spectacles"—"templum cui subiecimus gradus spectaculorum" (*De Spect.* 10. 5)—and it is this viewpoint which furnishes a characterization of the type of architectural model from which Pompey may have drawn. The search for temples under which steps were placed to serve for spectacles leads to several Italian buildings, and especially to three sanctuaries in Latium: at Gabii, Tibur, and Praeneste.

Some distance from the Acropolis of Gabii, near the Via Praenestina where the forum of the later city lay, are the remains of a sanctuary of the early second century

---

[1] See A. W. Pickard-Cambridge, *The Theatre of Dionysus in Athens*, pp. 1-10, for the earliest stage of the theater, with plan, p. 7, fig. 6. For the "Periclean" reconstruction, see pp. 15-16 with plan, fig. 7.

[2] They are closest at Cyrene and Syracuse. For the former see the plan in Luigi Pernier, *Il tempio e l'altare di Apollo a Cirene*, tav. 1. The theater lies just below the end of the long terrace on which the sanctuary is located, some 150 meters from the temple. The temple faces away from the theater, and the boundary wall of the *temenos* proper is about forty meters from the steps which lead down to the side of the *cavea*. In the case of Syracuse, G. E. Rizzo writes, "Questo abbiamo certo: che il recinto sacro [of Apollo] si stendeva, in parte, sulla terrazza soprastante al teatro, che il teatro era, senza alcun dubbio, in intima correlazione topografica col témenos stesso, come è dimostrato dalla scala facile ed ampia intagliata nella roccia." (*Il teatro greco di Siracusa*, p. 32.) But the *temenos* apparently included no temple, according to the latest investigations.

B.C.[3] The *cella* walls of the temple are still standing to a considerable height, but the adjuncts of the temple are for the most part destroyed or reburied, and one must depend on older descriptions and excavations for a reconstruction (Fig. 5).[4] The temple stands approximately in the center of a long rectangular *temenos*. Facing inward along each side of the *temenos* wall is a row of one-room shops, beginning opposite the front wall of the *cella* and continuing back to the rear wall of the precinct. A single colonnade runs along this rear wall and in front of the shops. There is a somewhat monumental entrance to the area from the rear, apparently leading onto the road which connected the Via Labicana with the Via Praenestina and crossed the Gabian acropolis. The side walls of the precinct, unadorned with shops or colonnade, continue to the front of the area, but the entire front face of the *temenos* is taken up by a monumental semicircular staircase whose maximum diameter approaches sixty meters, with approximately twelve rows of steps or seats leading up to the level of the temple podium.[5] The orchestra-like area determined by the semicircle of the lowest step is further bounded by a straight wall parallel to that part of the front *temenos* wall which limits the stairs, but several feet beyond it and tied to it by short side walls. A very small fragment of this wall is still visible at the surface of the ground.[6] Its position would correspond to that of the *scaenae frons* in a regular theater. Although neither its height nor details of its plan can be determined, Delbrueck rightly remarks that its presence precludes the possibility that the semicircular staircase is a mere monumental entry to the temple area,[7] although there may have been breaks in the wall that allowed it to be used also as an entrance, in addition to the approach from behind the temple. In all likelihood these remains belong to some sort of stage building and the steps are a theatrical *cavea* from which spectators could watch *spectacula* developed below.[8] Whether these were the ordinary *spectacula* of the Roman theater or special ceremonies connected with the cult of the divinity worshiped in the temple is im-

[3] The only modern publication is in Richard Delbrueck, *Hellenistische Bauten in Latium*, II, 5-10. Criteria for dating are only approximate, but his dating to ca. 200 B.C. seems probable and has not been questioned.

[4] One may conveniently refer to G. Pinza, "Gabii ed i suoi monumenti," *BullComm*, XXXI (1903), 330-343; and A. Nibby, *Analisi storico-topografico-antiquaria della carta de' dintorni di Roma*, II, 83-85. Earlier bibliography cited in Delbrueck, II, 5-6.

[5] Only the slope of the ground now reveals the semicircular steps. Visconti (*Monumenti Gabini della Villa Pinciana*, I, 16, quoted by Delbrueck, II, 7, n. 1) characterizes the remains as "vaghissima ed ampia gradinata che si ritira in dentro a foggia di semicircolo." Subsequent writers follow his plan, Delbrueck (II, 5) characterizing his book as "wichtig, weil Visconti mehr sah als jetzt da ist und ausführlich beschreibt." I have found no dimensions given for the individual steps.

[6] Observed by the writer in February 1955.

[7] "[Visconti] hielt das Theater für eine Freitreppe, womit die Reste des Bühnengebäudes nicht wohl zu vereinigen sind." (II, 7)

[8] Paolino Mingazzini ("Cagliari—resti di santuario punico e di altri ruderi a monte di Piazza del Carmine," *NSc*, Ser. VIII, Vol. III [1949], 226) wrongly considers the existence of a stage building doubtful and states further that the north-south direction of the *cavea* "sarebbe un argomento contro l'ipotesi teatrale," an argument which is certainly without force for a monument whose orientation would be determined by the temple, not the theatrical exedra. In any case there was never any real consistency in the orientation of ancient theaters.

possible to determine. In any case, the two elements were planned and built at a single stroke and their connection is indisputable. Architecturally, the temple stands above and behind the theater, dominating it on its central axis. The semicircular staircase serves simultaneously the function of a monumental approach leading the eye and feet up to the temple and a *theatron*, from which a large group of people can most efficiently watch events below. An "actor" on the stage would look directly up to the *cella* of the temple, and a priest standing in the doorway of the temple would look directly down on the stage. We do not know what divinity was worshiped here, but there are indications that the *cella* was divided at the rear into three small chambers by wooden partitions,[9] which would lead one to suggest either the Capitoline triad or the triad of Ceres, Liber, and Libera. The older attribution to Juno seems now to be false.[10]

The sanctuary of Hercules Victor at Tivoli is closely parallel to the Gabii sanctuary in its main lines although the scheme has here been carried out on a larger scale and with more elaboration (Fig. 7).[11] The entire complex is built up on an imposing series of vaulted substructures. The temple proper is at the center of the back of the sacred area, which is rectangular with its long dimension perpendicular to the axis of the temple. The whole of the rear and the two sides are formed by a two-story double colonnade with open façade on both the inside and outside of the *temenos*. But the front, as at Gabii, is cut into by a large semicircular staircase of some twelve steps, centered on the line of the axis of the temple (Fig. 8).[12] The center of the top step is only a few feet from the foot of the rectilinear steps of the temple itself, which stands on a high podium. At the foot of the *cavea*-like stairs are the remains of a series of vaults which determined a level platform extending some distance beyond the edge of these stairs, and it is almost certain that a stage building stood on this platform. An inscription found in this area and generally believed to refer to the constructions of the sanctuary itself states that the *quattuorviri* were responsible for the following: "porticus p(edum) CCLX et exsedram et pronaon et porticum pone scaenam long(um) p(edum) CXL."[13] If this inscription does refer to the sanctuary of Hercules Victor—and there are no other known buildings in the vicinity to which the terms in the text can be attributed—one must reconstruct a stage building of some sort. *Scaena* will allow no

[9] Delbrueck, II, 8.

[10] *Ibid.*, p. 5.

[11] I was not able to gain permission to visit the remains of this sanctuary, which lie for the most part under a paper factory and are now considered "unsafe." No good publication of the complex exists, but fortunately the available evidence has been restudied, and a great deal of what can be known has been included by Furio Fasolo and Giorgio Gullini in *Il santuario della Fortuna Primigenia a Palestrina* (see especially pp. 354-361, 424-433, and an excellent reconstruction, pl. XXIX.) One may also consult C. Carducci, *Tibur* ("Italia romana: municipi e colonie," Ser. I, Vol. III).

[12] As at Gabii, there seems to be no information on the size of individual steps, so one cannot infer whether they were meant for sitting or standing.

[13] *CIL*, XIV, 3664 = *Inscriptiones Italiae, Tibur*, n. 19. Discussed in Fasolo and Gullini, p. 432.

other meaning here.[14] Its logical position is in front of the *theatron* stairway, as in the structure at Gabii. A recent restudy of the remains by Fasolo led him to the conclusion that the vaulting at this point must in fact support something in the nature of a stage since there was no visible means of bridging the difference between ground level and the level of the platform in front of the semicircular stairs in order to render them usable as an entrance into the sanctuary.[15]

The same pattern of temple dominating theater steps recurs in a monument outside Latium on the edges of the Italic world. A recently excavated temple at Cagliari in Sardinia occupies the back of a rectangular *temenos* (Fig. 6).[16] The rectilinear staircase of the raised temple leads down onto a ring-shaped platform about 25 meters wide, at the edge of which begins the descent of a large semicircular staircase similar to the theater-like stairs at Gabii and Tivoli. The existence of eleven steps is sure, and two more must be added at the top to reach the level of the platform below the temple stairs. The *cavea* is carefully constructed of hard, high-quality limestone. The individual steps are 40 cm. high and 70 cm. wide, a size too large for comfortable use as stairs but corresponding well with the standard size for seats in the ancient theater. At two points smaller stairs were found inserted in the normal ones, as in the aisles of a theater *cavea*. Modern buildings have prevented the investigation of the area immediately below, so that the question of the presence or absence of a stage building to complete the complex can only be discussed in hypothetical terms, and the question is further complicated by the uncertainty as to both the date and the national type of the sanctuary complex.[17] Its excavator Mingazzini has made the interesting proposal that the structure is a purely Phoenician sanctuary from the late fourth or early third century B.C. Unfortunately the evidence seems insufficient to establish the likelihood of his identification, which would have provided us with virtually our only material manifestation of a native Punic sanctuary. The principal features of such a

[14] See Michaut, *Sur les tréteaux latins*, pp. 378-380, n. 1; and Albert Müller, "Untersuchungen zu den Bühnenalterthümern," *Philologus*, Suppl. VII (1899), 27-35.

[15] Fasolo and Gullini, p. 364, n. 5. He concludes that whatever entrances existed into the *temenos* must have been located at the sides of the front, beyond the semicircular stairs.

[16] Described in Mingazzini, *NSc*, Ser. VIII, Vol. III, 213-274; see especially pp. 224-229. A much clearer plan is given in Mingazzini, "Cagliari: ruderi di un santuario a Via Malta," *Le Arti*, II (1939-40), p. 59; reproduced in *AA*, LV (1940), 546, Abb. 55.

[17] Mingazzini (*NSc*, Ser. VIII, Vol. III, 225-226) lists four possibilities: (1) a full *scaena* as in a developed theater, (2) a simple low platform, (3) an altar, and (4) nothing. His discussion of these is based largely on the undemonstrated assumption that the cult place is purely Phoenician. Allowing no middle course between the full Hellenistic *scaena* and a low narrow platform, he rejects the former on the grounds that it is too "classical" for a Phoenician monument and the latter on the grounds that it is too small for the performance of the "scene sacre" which he hypothesizes for the cult. In addition, both, he states, "avrebbe compromesso grandemente il solenne effetto che da esso ci si riprometteva, come accesso al santuario divino." But this is not a convincing argument in the light of the well-documented structures at Tivoli and Gabii which *did* compromise the visual effect of the semicircular stairs as entrance. I see no reason why the hypothesis of some fairly substantial stage need be rejected, until excavation can complete the picture with certainty.

sanctuary are admitted to be a large open courtyard and a small *sanctum sanctorum* standing in the middle of this court.[18] In no case are we led to believe that the *naos* was a dominating feature, as it most decidedly and pointedly is in the Cagliari sanctuary, despite Mingazzini's strange observation that it occupies a relatively small position in respect to the sacred area.[19] If there were a high degree of probability in favor of a date around 300 B.C., one would, of course, have to admit its Punic character, but the evidence of finds apparently only establishes a *terminus post quem* of ca. 300 B.C. and a *terminus ante quem* of ca. 50 B.C. for activity on the site.[20] The natural activity which must have followed the organization of Sardinia as a Roman province in 238 would lead one to favor a late third or early second century date. On such an assumption, the "Italic" qualities of the sanctuary—its axiality and frontality, the dominance of the temple to which the eye is led by the two sets of stairs, in short, its striking parallels with the Tivoli and Gabii monuments described above—are natural, and, although one is surprised to see them manifested monumentally as far from Latium as Cagliari, the embarrassment to the architectural historian is far less than would be the positing of a heretofore unparalleled pre-Roman Punic form. As for the presence of a stage building, one can at most and should at least admit the possibility that some sort of platform or *scaena* existed in correspondence with similar elements at Gabii and Tivoli. Again we are at a loss to specify the type of *spectacula* for which the theater-like structure served, nor, as at Gabii, do we know the divinity to whom the sanctuary was sacred.[21] The Phoenician background of the site may not, of course, be disregarded even though one cannot admit that the architectural conception is Phoenician. Certain Syrian-Phoenician cults are known to have made use of a ritual "theater."[22] The sanctuary at Cagliari may be connected with such a cult, possibly in a Romanized form. But it must strongly be emphasized here, as in the somewhat similar situation in North Africa discussed below, that the evidence does not justify the conclusion that we are in the presence of a non-Italic architectural form, but only suggests that a non-Italic religious tradition may help to explain, *in this one instance*, the adoption and use of the type of temple-theater complex in question.

A fourth monument which bears close relations to the three temple areas described above is the sanctuary of Fortuna Primigenia at Praeneste, the subject of intensive study, publication, and reconstruction since World War II, when bombs and shells did much to clear off mediaeval and later houses from the skeleton of the upper portion of the Roman structure.[23] The sanctuary as a whole is built up on a steep

[18] See Mingazzini, *NSc*, Ser. VIII, Vol. III, 223-224, and the bibliography there cited.
[19] *Ibid.*, p. 224.
[20] *Ibid.*
[21] *Ibid.*, pp. 228-229. The weakness of the "evidence" here adduced is immediately apparent, as the writer himself states.
[22] These took several different forms. See below, pp. 65-68, where the phenomenon is discussed in detail.
[23] The results are visible in the monograph of Fasolo and Gullini, *Il santuario della Fortuna Primigenia a Palestrina*. Previous bibliography will be found in their notes, p. 14.

series of terraces whose function, reduced to simplest terms, is to connect a lower cult place to an upper cult place. The whole is unified on an axis through ramps and staircases whose visual effect is to point toward and accentuate the top of the complex, the portion pertinent to this study (Fig. 9).[24] The shrine at the summit, hidden today inside a baronial palace, is a small circular "tholos" cut partly into the native rock of the hillside, perhaps a regularization of an earlier "cave" shrine like the one on the bottom level of the sanctuary (Figs. 10 and 11).[25] Its façade is hidden however, since the "tholos" is joined by a narrow entrance to the center of a large curved double colonnade, not quite a full semicircle, from which descends a *cavea*-like staircase of seventeen steps ending in a relatively small "orchestra," 10.5 meters wide at the front. There is an immediate drop, however, of 6.6 meters to the next level of the sanctuary complex, an immense rectangular piazza surrounded on three sides by a double colonnade.[26] Although the architectural remains are scarce at this point, Fasolo and Gullini's reconstruction of the connection between these two levels fits these remains best and must be considered the most likely solution.[27] They consider that a single rectilinear staircase descended from the edge of the platform at the foot of the theater-like exedra out into the piazza below. It was on the central axis, so that it would be possible to walk in a straight line from the center of the front of that piazza—the point, in fact, where one would enter the piazza through the ramps from below—up to the shrine at the summit. The semicircular *"cavea"* is therefore quite pointless as a purely functional staircase to approach the temple. On the other hand, it seems equally useless as a theater in the ordinary sense of the word, since there is no possibility of completing it with either stage building or platform, and the "orchestra" is too small for the development of any elaborate spectacle. Keeping in view the limitations in space and visibility imposed by the changes in level, one may conceive three different ways in which the steps could still function as a sort of *theatron*.[28] A simple ceremony or sacrifice or speech could be performed in the top "orchestra" and witnessed by a fairly

[24] See especially Fasolo and Gullini, fig. 333, p. 248; fig. 461, p. 343; fig. 464d, p. 347; tav. III and XII.

[25] *Ibid.*, pp. 183-192 and tav. IV, for a detailed description of the remains of this top portion. The following summary (pp. 191-192) is important: ". . . il grande emiciclo superiore, con l'ambiente che si apre sul fondo, doveva essere la parte più riservata, con la statua di culto, destinata alle cerimonie. Infatti anche nell'ambiente definito non molto chiaramente sul fondo dell'emiciclo, doveva affiorare la roccia che abbiamo visto avere sempre una parte notevole nei luoghi più sacri del culto della Fortuna. È facile quindi immaginare che proprio al sommo di tutto il complesso superiore ci fosse un centro religioso analogo a quello che troviamo nella parte inferiore nel gruppo tra l'antro delle sorti e la sala absidata. Non possiamo certo precisare le eventuali differenze tra i due centri, differenze di cerimonie o di particolari aspetti della divinità ivi venerata; comunque possiamo assicurare la destinazione al culto del grande emiciclo superiore."

[26] Called "la terrazza della 'cortina' " by Fasolo and Gullini; described in full, *ibid.*, pp. 167-183.

[27] *Ibid.*, pp. 169-170. They rightly reject a system corresponding to the two baroque ramps converging on the axis, which provided the connection before they were destroyed in World War II. These would have cut across and rendered useless the open vaulted rooms below.

[28] An excellent idea of the lines of vision from various parts of this upper area can be gained from Fasolo and Gullini, fig. 462, p. 345.

extensive number of spectators standing on the steps and in the portico above. Such a ceremony could be seen even from the front of the round shrine. A more extensive ceremony or pageant or play could be performed on the rectangular piazza below, and, as long as the action was restricted approximately to the front half of that piazza—an area about 100 meters long and 25 meters wide—the ceremony could be witnessed by spectators in the exedra above, with room for other spectators at the back of the piazza itself out of the line of vision from above. A third possibility is that the *"spectaculum"* itself may have taken place on the semicircular stairs and colonnade, in the form of an array of important personages, priests and officials, who would thus be made eminently visible to persons on the lower terraces of the sanctuary. (Fig. 11, a photograph taken from the point of view of a spectator on the piazza immediately below the "theater.")[29] Despite the impossibility of determining the exact use of this *cavea* at Palestrina, it is highly probable that the steps were employed for *spectacula* of some nature. However, even if they are purely decorative it does not detract from their aptness as a model for the later Roman combination of temple and theater, since this semicircular exedra suggests at least the appearance of a theater. The suggestion is even more striking because of the portico above the top row of steps, corresponding closely to the portico which regularly crowns the *cavea* of the fully developed Roman theater building.[30] It is interesting to note further that at Palestrina the temple itself, though its central position is clear from the ground plan, does not physically dominate the monument by means of its superstructure. It is rather hidden behind the whole façade of the colonnade surmounting the *cavea*.[31] The center of the curve of the auditorium is accented by the lines of the whole symmetrical complex, and probably not by any extra weight or height visible from below, a feature which would correspond with some of the later examples of the Roman theater shrine.[32]

The traditional dating of this important structure is "Sullan," specifically referring to the period immediately following the damages undergone by the city in the civil fighting of 82 B.C. Fasolo and Gullini, who have studied the monument in detail during the recent excavations and restorations, insist that the sanctuary is considerably earlier in concept and construction, dating from ca. 150 B.C., and that the Sullan work is mostly limited to repairs on the lower half.[33] Their deductions have been called into question by Lugli.[34] For the purposes of the present discussion it is

[29] This last is the solution imagined by Fasolo and Gullini, p. 192: "La sua posizione e la grande scalea che si affaccia verso la sottostante piazza dovevano consentire ad una massa notevole di fedeli di assistere alle cerimonie. Dobbiamo infatti immaginare la folla raccolta nella piazza corrispondente all'attuale cortina e i sacerdoti collocati nell'interno dell'emiciclo o sulla scalinata semicircolare in modo da essere pienamente visibili da tutti i fedeli."

[30] Margarete Bieber, *The History of the Greek and Roman Theater*, ch. 14.

[31] Fasolo and Gullini, p. 191. The portico itself at the top of the stairs rose to a height approximately equal to the present façade of the palace. See fig. 497, p. 405.

[32] E.g., at Dugga. See fig. 24.

[33] Fasolo and Gullini, pp. 301-336.

[34] Giuseppe Lugli, "Il santuario della Fortuna prenestina e la sua datazione," *RendLinc*, Ser.

of minor importance which date is accepted although the weight of the evidence is slightly greater on the side of the earlier date. In either case the association of Sulla with the site remains, through his repairs to the lower sanctuary and his planting of a *colonia* at Praeneste,[35] and underlines the importance of the monument in the period immediately preceding Pompey's building activities. Both this sanctuary and the temple of Hercules Victor at Tibur, constructed even nearer in date to Rome's first stone theater,[36] must have been regarded as architectural landmarks, and were before the eyes of the Romans as impressive building achievements in cities which they constantly visited.

The term Hellenistic has been firmly affixed to these monuments, as it is affixed to the title page of Delbrueck's *Hellenistische Bauten in Latium*. One of the major purposes of Fasolo and Gullini in their publication of the Palestrina sanctuary has been to dislodge "Hellenistic" in favor of "Italic."[37] What they mean by this term in this context—what one must necessarily mean by it in this period—is not "non-Hellenistic," but rather the particular direction which the fluid experimentation of the Hellenistic world took in Italy, as partly determined by localized pre-Hellenistic forms and concepts, more strictly to be called "Italic." Among the latter the commonplaces are axiality and frontality. A more difficult concept to manipulate is "la sensibilità per uno spazio concreto," sensibility toward a concrete—i.e., defined and limited—space.[38] In the particular architectural problem with which this chapter deals it is of importance to emphasize the "Italic" derivation of the form, since we can find no example of a *theatron* appended in like manner to a temple in the Hellenistic sphere outside Italy. The closest approach, that of the theater at Pergamon, still retains an accidental quality which renders it essentially different architecturally—and, one is tempted to say, ideologically—from the examples in Italy. At Pergamon the theater was constructed on the slope under the terrace which contained the temple of Athena, but neither centered with respect to the sanctuary nor facing the front of the temple, and the temple was hidden from the theater by a colonnade later erected at the edge of the *temenos* overlooking the theater.[39] A narrow staircase led between the two but was distinctly of an incidental quality.[40]

VIII, Vol. IX (1954), 51-87. Answered by Giorgio Gullini, "Ancora sul santuario della Fortuna Primigenia a Palestrina," *ArchCl*, VI (1954), 133-147.

[35] See Carolina Lanzani, *Lucio Cornelio Silla Dittatore*, pp. 55-60, 143.

[36] Dated in the decade 70-60 B.C. See Fasolo and Gullini, pp. 424-425.

[37] *Ibid.*, pp. 441-455.

[38] *Ibid.*, p. 450.

[39] See Richard Bohn, *Das Heiligtum der Athena Polias Nikephoros* ("Altertümer von Pergamon," II), pp. 2 and 28, with pl. III.

[40] Richard Bohn, *Die Theater-Terrasse* ("Altertümer von Pergamon," IV), p. 17 and pl. I.
More interesting is the connection between the theater and the small Ionic temple closing the end of the narrow terrace behind the stage and facing along the axis of the terrace toward the stage building and the *parodoi* (*Ibid.*, pp. 41-71). It or the so-called *Nischenbau* on the same terrace (*Ibid.*, pp. 18-20) is probably associated with the Pergamene ruler cult, and referred to in an inscription found in Teos as τὸ Ἀττάλειον τὸ πρὸς τῷ θεάτρῳ, ὃ καὶ ζῶν καθιερώκει τοῖς Ἀτταλισταῖς.

The same architectural pattern of theater-like steps dominated by an important building can be found in the Roman world in quite another context, the political meeting place. Recent excavations by the American Academy in Rome at Cosa have unearthed a building complex which has been interpreted, with great probability, as the *comitium* and *curia* of the colony (Fig. 12).[41] It dates from the third century B.C. and lies on the northeast side of the forum, between the basilica and the large forum temple known as Temple B. Its position is important in establishing the identity of the structure, since it lies directly opposite the point from which the main road, coming from the sacred area on the *arx*, enters the forum. Directly off the forum is an unroofed rectangular area, 19 by 17½ meters, completely enclosed by a wall except for a narrow entrance at the center of the front. In the middle of this area is a circular pavement, 8.6 meters in diameter, with a round depression at its exact center which may have served as the setting for a small altar. Except at the entrance, this "orchestra" was surrounded by steep steps, parts of which have been preserved. There were approximately eight steps, each 33 centimeters high and 40 centimeters wide, a size designed for standing rather than sitting. The capacity of the auditorium may be estimated at about 500. Centered at the back of this theater-like room is a simple rectangular building approximately 7 by 10 meters, whose front wall is identical with the back wall of the court. A lower foundation story is hidden from the front, as the ground slopes rapidly away from the forum, but the main story rose above the auditorium in front. The rectangular building is not a temple, and since the area below is an obvious *theatron* the most logical interpretation of the ruins is to regard it as a *curia* closely attached to an open-air meeting place serving the function of a *comitium*. If this view is correct, we have the following general plan for a Roman political meeting place: the *comitium* resembles a small theater in which the speakers stood in the orchestra and the listeners stood in the *cavea*. Above and behind the assembly place rose the meeting place of the *decuriones* in such a way that the *cavea* of the *comitium* was at the same time the front steps of the *curia*. Such a general arrangement does not in fact seem surprising in the

---

(*CIG*, II, 3069, lines 20-21). The archaeological evidence for buildings devoted to the Hellenistic ruler cults is slight. (See Erich Boehringer and Friedrich Krauss, *Das Temenos für den Herrscherkult* ["Altertümer von Pergamon," IX], pp. 81-94, especially p. 88.) Nevertheless, this one instance of topographical collocation is perhaps to be interpreted in the light of the use made of the Dionysiac *technitai* by Hellenistic rulers in connection with ceremonies of the dynastic cult. (See Rostovtzeff, *The Social and Economic History of the Hellenistic World*, II, 1048-50; and Poland in *RE*, A5, cols. 2473ff., *s.v.* "technitai.") Consequently, the architectural connection at Pergamon may not be accidental and may reflect a more general Hellenistic use of the theater and its environs for dynastic propaganda.

[41] Excavated in May-June 1954, under the direction of Dr. Lawrence Richardson, Jr., field archaeologist of the American Academy in Rome. A preliminary publication of the findings may be seen in Lawrence Richardson, Jr., "Cosa and Rome: Comitium and Curia," *Archaeology*, X (1957), 49-55. The following paragraphs are substantially a condensation of an unpublished lecture given by the writer in November 1954, at the American Academy: "L'ultima stagione di scavi—comizio e curia."

light of the form of the *comitium* at Rome itself, a natural model for the colony to follow.

Only recently has a general view of the pattern of the Roman *comitium* been formulated on the basis of sound archaeological investigation.[42] The language of Professor Sjöqvist's description of the site at Rome, written before the discovery at Cosa, is of extreme pertinence both to a confirmation of the Cosan monument's character and the general problem of this chapter.

The arrangement and planning of the Comitium was from the beginning determined by the configuration of the terrain. The hillslope to the North of the Forum was limited by two converging roads and formed *a concave theatre-like sector.* This was the seating place of the people, covering an area of about 2,900 square meters and thus accommodating more than 5,800 people. To judge from independent literary evidence the *cavea* must—at least during some period of its long life—have been partly or totally provided with steps for the comfort of the audience. We know also that on certain occasions it could temporarily be partly roofed in, probably by large awnings (Livy 27. 36. 8), a system well known from later evidence regarding theatre performances. . . . *Dominating the Comitium, at the top of the cavea* and probably oriented North-South lay the old Curia, looking down over the meeting place and facing the Rostra to the South. . . . The Comitium was easily accessible from the Forum area and from the two main arteries bordering the "saeptum," probably by an open entrance on each side of the Rostra, placed *like the "parodoi" of a theatre.* The area could of course also be reached from above by way of the Curia, which was in direct communication with the Comitium.[43]

In addition, certain ancient sources themselves speak of the area in terms which suggest the analogy between *comitium* and theater. In Livy's description of the murder of Servius Tullius by Tarquinius Superbus (i. 48. 3), Tarquinius picks up his son-in-law and "e curia in inferiorem partem per gradus deiecit." The sector is definitely spoken of as "stepped," and the analogy with the theater is helped by the fact that *gradus* is a specific term for the seats in a theater.[44] In the Greek version of the story by Dionysius of Halicarnassus the word κρηπίδες is used, which is unexampled as a straight flight of steps leading up to a building but possible in the sense of theatrical seats.[45] Another passage in Livy (i. 36. 5) locates a statue of Attus Navius "in comitio in gradibus ipsis ad laevam curiae," with a similar suggestion in the word *gradus.*

The Cosa complex of *comitium* and *curia* does not appear to be unique. At Paestum, on the north side of the Roman forum beside the "Temple of Peace," lies a monument usually referred to in the guidebooks as the "so-called theater" (Fig. 14).[46] In its original form it is likely that the "theater" was a complete circle of steps, with a

---

[42] By Erik Sjöqvist in "Pnyx and Comitium," *Studies Presented to David Moore Robinson,* I, 400-411. Earlier views and bibliography in Giuseppe Lugli, *Monumenti minori del Foro romano,* pp. 1-27.

[43] *Studies Presented to David Moore Robinson,* I, 405-406. The italics are mine.

[44] *ThLL, s.v.*

[45] Sjöqvist, *Studies Presented to David Moore Robinson,* I, 405. See *L.-S.-J., s.v.,* II, 2.

[46] See P. C. Sestieri, *Paestum,* p. 22; Touring Club Italiano, *Guida d'Italia—Napoli e dintorni,* p. 523.

[47] No published study of the building exists. For the following interpretation I depend on

diameter about twice as great as that at Cosa.[47] The steps, about the same height as those in the Cosan *comitium*, are somewhat wider. There were eight rows. The main entrance was on the south, or forum, side. Back of the round theater and raised above it is a row of five parallel halls, simple rectangular rooms with a single façade which would be tangent to the top of the circle of steps, if we suppose that it was originally a complete circle. It is likely that these are the *curia* and subsidiary buildings of the Roman colony, and that the theater in front is that colony's *comitium*. The parallel is extremely striking in view of the fact that at a later period at Cosa a room was constructed on either side of the *curia* so that the façade of the back building extended along the whole of the back of the *comitium* (Fig. 13), and also in view of the fact that the two colonies have the same foundation date, 273 B.C.

One of the forms of a Roman *curia* and *comitium*, then, provides a further example of curved steps serving simultaneously as the entrance to an important building and as a *theatron*.[48] It should be added to the list of those Italic models available to the eye of Pompey's architect when he set out to "place a theater under a temple."

---

data furnished by Dr. Lawrence Richardson, Jr., who made measurements and archaeological soundings there in May 1955, on behalf of the American Academy in Rome and with the permission of the Italian government.

[48] It is interesting to note that the *curia*, in Rome, at least, was inaugurated as a *templum*, making the parallel more literally exact. (See Hülsen in *RE*, IV, col. 1822, *s.v.* "Curia, 4d.") Further weight is perhaps added to the parallel by the political significance attached to the theater as a gathering place of the masses. (See below, p. 48) It is impossible, however, to follow Richardson (*Archaeology*, X, 53) in making this the exclusive model for the theater of Pompey.

CHAPTER III

THE THEATER OF POMPEY

"Pompeius Magnus, solo theatro suo minor . . ." (Tert. *De Spect.* 10. 5)

THE THEATER OF POMPEY

THE CENTRAL POSITION which Pompey's theater holds in this study is justified not only by its religious connections, but also by its own prominence in the eyes of the Romans as the first monumental Roman theater. Immense, dominating all the buildings around it, it was for over forty years the only stone theater in Rome. Even after others were constructed, it remained the most important and the porticoes and gardens around it made it one of the city's showplaces.[1] It was continually restored and renovated late into the Empire.[2]

Pompey built it at the height of his career. Plutarch gives an account of its conception as the victorious general was returning from his campaigns against Mithridates:

> After he had set everything in order, he journeyed homeward with great pomp and festivity: when he came to Mytilene, he gave the city its freedom upon the intercession of Theophanes, and was present at the traditional contest of the poets, who took at that time no other theme or subject than the actions of Pompey. He was extremely pleased with the theater itself, and had a model of it taken, intending to erect one in Rome on the same design, but larger and more magnificent.[3]

It was dedicated in 55 B.C. and the *ludi* were appropriately grand.[4]

Although much of the structure of the theater and surroundings probably remains under the present houses and streets, and the over-all form of the theater can be clearly traced in the pattern of the buildings in and near the Piazza di S. Maria di Grottapinta, very little of the actual construction can now be seen.[5] Fortunately, however, practically the entire Pompeian complex is covered by extant fragments of the Severan marble plan (Fig. 15).[6] Adding the evidence from literary references, one can be absolutely certain of the location, the general plan, and some architectural details of this important building (Figs. 1 and 16).

It is located in the southern part of the Campus Martius, just west of the already constructed Circus Flaminius and south of the later stadium of Domitian. The general

---

[1] Incidental references to the theater of Pompey and its porticoes are unusually frequent in Imperial literature: e.g., Tac. *Ann.* xiii. 54; Martial *Epig.* ii. 14. 10; vi. 9; x. 51. 11; xiv. 29. 1; xiv. 166. 1; Propertius ii. 32. 11-12; iv. 8. 75; Ov. *Ars Am.* i. 67; iii. 387. Even after two other permanent theaters were built in Rome, it could be called simply "theatrum": Suet. *Ner.* 13; Florus ii. 13. 91; Cass. Dio l. 8. 3. Ammianus Marcellinus still referred to it "inter decora Urbis" (xvi. 10. 14).

[2] We know of restorations under Augustus, Tiberius and Claudius, Domitian, Severus, Diocletian, Arcadius, Honorius, and Symmachus. For sources see Platner-Ashby, *A Topographical Dictionary of Ancient Rome*, pp. 516-517, *s.v.* "Theatrum Pompei."

[3] καὶ γὰρ εἰς Μιτυλήνην ἀφικόμενος τήν τε πόλιν ἠλευθέρωσε διὰ Θεοφάνη, καὶ τὸν ἀγῶνα τὸν πάτριον ἐθεάσατο τῶν ποιητῶν, ὑπόθεσιν μίαν ἔχοντα τὰς ἐκείνου πράξεις. ἡσθεὶς δὲ τῷ θεάτρῳ περιεγράψατο τὸ εἶδος αὐτοῦ καὶ τὸν τύπον ὡς ὅμοιον ἀπεργασόμενος τὸ ἐν Ῥώμῃ, μεῖζον δὲ καὶ σεμνότερον. (*Vit. Pomp.* 42. 3)

[4] These are described by Cass. Dio xxxix. 38; Plin. *HN* viii. 7; and Cic. *Fam.* vii. 1, to Marius.

[5] Traces of the supporting arches and vaults of the *cavea* may be seen in most of the basements of the area, most easily in the Ristorante Pancrazio, but it is difficult to form a connected picture of the ruins. A fairly complete listing of the visible remains will be found in Colini, "Il problema archeologico del teatro di Pompeo," *Capitolium*, 1937, pp. 118-122.

[6] Fragment 30. See Jordan, *Forma urbis Romae*, 22-23. Reproduced in Bieber, *History*, fig. 630.

plan was the standard "Vitruvian" one, with semicircular *cavea* and orchestra closely connected to a long stage building.[7] The auditorium was large, with a diameter of approximately 150 meters and a capacity for between ten and twenty thousand spectators.[8] It was built up from level ground on a series of radiating walls crowned with vaults, and the construction where visible is solid and mostly finished with *opus quasi-reticulatum*. In short, it probably did not differ appreciably in appearance from the now visible theater of Marcellus, except in one important feature: it had one moderately large temple and four smaller shrines built into it.

According to Tertullian,[9] Pompey dedicated the whole structure as a temple of Venus, "cui subiecimus, inquit, gradus spectaculorum." Suetonius[10] mentions the several temples, calling them *superiores aedes*. The temples were at the top of the auditorium, then, and the *templum Veneris* must have been located on the central axis, since the marble plan has a representation at this point which is best interpreted as the foundations of a temple (Fig. 15),[11] and some remains of heavy walls perpendicular to the circumference wall of the *cavea* and at its midpoint were found under the Palazzo Pio Righetti in 1860, with fragments of engaged columns.[12] The temple extended some distance beyond the auditorium and had to be built up from the ground to the top of the *cavea* on its own foundations. The back ended in a semicircular apse. The arrangement of columns is uncertain, as is the appearance at the front where theater and temple came together. Because of its proportions, however, and the heaviness of the foundations, it seems likely that the elevation of the temple was sufficient

---

[7] In general, see Canina's restored plan and elevations originally published in his monograph *Ricerche iconografiche sul teatro di Pompeo e fabbriche adiacenti*; and reproduced in his *Gli edifizii di Roma antica*, IV, pls. CLIII-CLVIII, with text in Vol. III, pp. 7-18. A convenient modern reproduction of the plan is to be found in Bieber, *History*, fig. 631. Obviously this reconstruction, like any other, must be used with caution, and we cannot be certain of the superstructure until excavation has brought it to light. There is no necessity, however, to say with Lugli (*Monumenti antichi*, III, 74) that the *cavea* was perhaps only carried to a height of one or two orders of arcades. The designation of the theater as "magnum" (Plin. *HN* VII. 48. 158) while the theater of Marcellus was standing nearby to a height of three full stories, the capabilities and propensities of Roman building techniques of the time, and the large diameter of the theater all argue against this assumption.

[8] Pliny (*HN* XXXVI. 24. 115) quotes the capacity at 40,000, but modern scholarship has tended to lower all such figures to a carefully conservative number based on present per capita seating space allowances.

[9] *De Spect.* 10. 5.

[10] *Claud.* 21. 1.

[11] The iconography of the Severan map is disputed in many particulars. Here there are two parallel lines, not quite perpendicular to the curve representing the outside wall of the *cavea*. Along the outside of each line and touching it is a row of three dots inscribed in squares. These probably should be taken to indicate square pilasters at ground level which support columns at the level of the shrine, as in the representations of the temple of Hercules Musarum, fragment 33. The most difficult feature, however, is that the lines are not joined together at the back and there is no indication of the "apse" end of the temple. The fact that the façade of the temple is not represented is natural if the map represents the ground level plan.

[12] See Pellegrini, "Scavi di Roma," *BdI*, XXXVII (1865), 201-203.

to dominate whatever portico or colonnade crowned the *cavea* as a whole (Figs. 17 and 18).

What were the motives that induced Pompey, or his architect, to build this temple to Venus Victrix at the top of his monumental theater?

The standard attitude, from the time of Tertullian at the end of the second century, has been to make light of the shrine and its meaning and to speak of the "cynical shrewdness"[13] of Pompey in using a religious excuse to put across a purely political construction program. In the *De Spectaculis* (10. 5) Tertullian interprets Pompey's action in these words:

> When Pompey the Great had constructed that citadel of all vice, since he was afraid of a censorious punishment of his memory, he placed above it a shrine of Venus, and when he invited the people by proclamation to the dedication, he announced it not as a theater but as a temple of Venus, "under which," he said, "we have placed steps for watching games."[14]

A modern writer repeats Tertullian's explanation, calling it a "curious story": "The populace was invited to the dedication not of a theater but of a temple of Venus, to which, added Pompey *slyly*, I have appended seats for a theater. Of course, since the seats were there, fully constructed, *so practical a people as the Romans* did not allow them to remain unused."[15] A sentence of Alföldi's gives a somewhat different shading of the same idea:

> This temple erected over the rows of seats of the new theater gave the hypocrite Pompey the pretext to camouflage the colossal building complex of his permanent theater as a Venus-shrine.[16]

Andreas Rumpf emphasizes the political motives to such an extent that in a recent ten-page article on the development of the permanent theater building in Rome he fails completely to mention the shrine of Venus Victrix.[17] And there are other histories of the Roman theater where one may search in vain for any discussion of the temple.[18]

[13] The phrase is James Turney Allen's in *Stage Antiquities of the Greeks and Romans and their Influence*, p. 97.

[14] "Pompeius Magnus . . . cum illam arcem omnium turpitudinum extruxisset, veritus quandoque memoriae suae censoriam animadversionem Veneris aedem superposuit et ad dedicationem edicto populum convocans, non theatrum sed Veneris templum nuncupavit, cui subiecimus, inquit, gradus spectaculorum."

[15] Charles Knapp, "The Roman Theater," *Art and Archaeology*, I (1915), 138. The italics are mine.

[16] "Dieser Tempel, der über den Sitzstufen des neuen Theaters errichtet war, gab ja dem Heuchler Pompeius den Vorwand, den kolossalen Baukomplex seines—in Rom sittlich bedenklichen—ständigen Theaters als ein Venus-Heiligtum zu tarnen." ("Komplementare Doppeltypen in der Denarprägung der Römischen Republik," *Schweizer Münzblätter*, 1951, p. 3, cited by J. van Ooteghem, *Pompée le grand, bâtisseur d'empire*, p. 407, n. 2.)

[17] "Die Entstehung des Römischen Theaters," *MdI*, III (1950), 40-50. In a review of this article (*Dioniso*, XVII [1954], 171-177) Giacomo Caputo also notes and criticizes this omission. He says (p. 176), "Questo silenzio mi fa pensare che l'Autore non abbia tenuto nel dovuto conto il peso logico e critico di questa eccezionale particolarità."

[18] Bieber, however, now points up the "intimate relation" between the theater and the temple (*The History of the Greek and Roman Theater*, ch. 13).

That it must not be considered so lightly is apparent first of all from a consideration of ancient references. If we remove the inferences of Tertullian from the citation above we are still left with the statement of Pompey himself that he meant his building to be taken as a temple "cui subiecimus gradus spectaculorum." Before we scoff at this statement, armed with our modern conception of the sophisticated Roman politician, it deserves at least the chance to be examined as a serious statement of intent, especially as it is reiterated in an anecdote related by Gellius. He tells of a grammatical discussion in which the question is whether one should write "consul tertium" or "consul tertio"; Tiro is quoted as stating that Pompey had the same problem "when he was about to dedicate the temple of Victory, whose steps also would serve in place of a theater."[19] Furthermore, the elder Pliny, in describing the splendid ceremonies at the dedication of the building, remains true to the spirit of Pompey's expressed intent in that he does not even mention the theater but refers to the proceedings as the "dedicatio templi Veneris Victricis."[20] The actions of Claudius when he rededicated the theater demonstrate that he at least was convinced of the significance of the temple: "He conducted the games at the dedication of the theater of Pompey, which he had restored after a fire, from a tribunal placed in the orchestra, after he had first made supplication at the shrines on top and walked down the middle of the *cavea* through the silent seated crowd."[21] Nor is the temple itself lost sight of in incidental references, even in the thirteenth century, when one of the *Mirabilia* states, "ad concam Parionis fuit templum Cnei Pompei."[22]

Of modern writers who have treated the theater of Pompey, Marchetti-Longhi has given the most attention to problems of religion.[23] In a series of monographs on the topography of the area surrounding the three permanent theaters of Rome, he has deluged readers with evidence for the existence of dozens of little-known cults. His statements have aroused violent opposition, particularly at the hands of the encyclopaedic topographer Lugli.[24] Because of their importance for this study, Marchetti-Longhi's views are here outlined insofar as they pertain to the theater of Pompey.

1. The attribution of the founding of permanent theaters to private initiative and liberality is completely false.

[19] "Cum aedem Victoriae dedicaturus foret, cuius gradus vicem theatri essent." Gell. *NA* x. 1. 6-7. Incidentally, Pompey is said to have solved the problem by writing "TERT."

[20] Plin. *HN* viii. 7.

[21] "Ludos dedicationis Pompeiani theatri, quod ambustum restituerat, e tribunali posito in orchestra commisit, cum prius apud superiores aedes supplicasset perque mediam caveam sedentibus ac silentibus cunctis descendisset." Suet. *Claud.* 21. 1.

[22] Urlichs, *Cod. Top. Urbis Romae*, p. 107. An earlier reference is in Porphyrio's commentary on Horace (*Sat.* i. 2. 94), describing a certain Catia as "adeo vilis ut in aede Veneris theatri Pompeiani adulterium . . . admiserit."

[23] For a list of all his principal articles touching the subject, see the Bibliography. His views are perhaps best stated in the most recent: "Religione e teatro, l'influenza religiosa nella costruzione e nella topografia dei teatri nell'antica Roma," *ArchEspArq*, XXVI (1953), 3-37.

[24] See especially Giuseppe Lugli, "L'origine dei teatri stabili in Roma antica secondo i recenti studi," *Dioniso*, IX (1942), 55-64.

2. The connection of theatrical performances with religion is not only basic, but also lasting and specific: that it is lasting is proved by the fact that Pompey, in the middle of the first century b.c., could justify his theater *solely* on religious grounds; that it is specific is proved by the fact that Rome abounds in hillsides which would have made theater construction much easier if the cults had been appropriate, but all three permanent theaters were instead constructed in the Campus Martius because of the pre-existence there of cults especially asssociated with *ludi scaenici*.

3. The cult of Venus Victrix created *ex novo* would not sufficiently justify the theater of Pompey because it did not have sufficient associations with *ludi scaenici*. The same is true of the four divinities honored in the smaller shrines.

4. But there were other cults in the area which did justify the construction of the theater, viz. (a) Flora, manifested in the Floralia. Its presence is to be inferred from the mediaeval name of the Campo de' Fiori and the general swampy nature of the area in early times. (b) An Italic cult of Apollo, as opposed to the Hellenistic cult centered at the temple of Apollo Sosianus. Its existence is inferred mainly from ancient confusions between "Veiovis" and "Apollo" and from interpretations of various references *ad Apollinis* in Livy. It is localized in Temple C of the Area Sacra dell'Argentina. (c) Some pre-existing cult of Venus, manifested in the Vinalia and perhaps identifiable with the cult of Venus Erycina. A cult of Venus Victrix could not be sufficiently explained "in rapporto a Pompeo ed alla sua gens, di origine plebea e di lustro recente,"[25] and there is no written evidence for its invention by Pompey. Furthermore the previous presence of a cult of Venus is inferred from supposed traces of an earlier temple seen in 1864, and from analogy with the cult of Venus Murcia in the valley of the Circus Maximus.

Although Marchetti-Longhi's views are important and emphasize the factor of religion which is the subject of the present study, they cannot be accepted without criticism.

He goes too far in denying completely the political and personal motives which governed the founding of Pompey's theater.[26] Pompey was in many respects the heir of Sulla. One of the things he must have inherited was the concept of public works as a means of political propaganda and personal glorification, a concept which is usually said to have been inaugurated by Caesar and Augustus. The Tabularium at Rome and the systematization of the great sanctuary at Palestrina[27] are in this sense forerunners of Pompey's theater group. In this, as in his attempts to bring religious concepts into close association with his political ambitions, Pompeius Magnus far

---

[25] " 'Theatrum lapideum,' 'Curia Pompeia,' e 'Trullum Dominae Maraldae,' " *RendPontAcc*, Ser. iii, Vol. xii (1936), 242.

[26] He condemns those who might suggest political motives "proiettando nel periodo republicano un opportunismo politico che, se mai, serà proprio solo del periodo imperiale." (*ArchEspArq*, xxvi, 11) However, any study of the political activity of the late Republic leads us to believe that "opportunism" was not a new invention of Augustan politics.

[27] See above, pp. 35-36.

surpassed Sulla Felix and showed the way to the emperors. The theater itself might be explained on religious grounds alone, but not so the immense group of monuments which surrounded it and made it one of the most famous public showplaces: the gardens and porticoes, the *hecatostylon*, and the much debated *curia*.[28]

In this connection, too, one may criticize Marchetti-Longhi's contention that the location of Pompey's theater, as well as the two other permanent theaters, in the Campus Martius area proves the *specific* nature of the connection between cult and theater. Of course he is right when he says that there were many hillsides in Rome where a theater could have been built in or near the sacred *temenos* of the divinities worshiped on those hills. In fact we know of one theater which was actually built on the slope of the Palatine in addition to dramatic performances given on the crest of the Palatine for the *ludi Megalenses*.[29] But the theaters of Pompey and Marcellus and Balbus (especially that of Pompey) could not have been built on these hillsides, because they included as part of their plans "public amusement parks," of such an extent that the level and little-inhabited Campus Martius was the only practical ground on which to build them (Figs. 1 and 19). Marchetti-Longhi also tacitly assumes that the Romans would have chosen the more conventional and cheaper "Greek" method of utilizing the natural *cavea* of a hillside for their theaters if some religious motive had not prevented this. But the Romans were just beginning to discover the monumental possibilities of the vault, and in any case conventionality and economy were seldom their guiding motivations in architecture. Reasoning more in accordance with the times would lead one to say that Pompey constructed his theater on the level ground of the Campus Martius partly because this was in fact more difficult, more expensive, and more showy. The same reasoning would hold good for Augustus and his supporter Balbus. Marchetti-Longhi's view on this point also, incidentally, deprives Pompey of any credit for the advancement in city planning for which his utilization of the Campus Martius was responsible. It enabled the increasingly crowded public activity of the city to spread out, and provided, in effect, a new forum area which was later connected to the old Forum Romanum by the chain of Imperial fora.

One other factor which should be remembered in modifying Marchetti-Longhi's contention is the striking use of the theater in the last decades of the Republic as a political sounding block. Cicero remarks in his oration for Sestius that the judgment and desires of the Roman people may be made apparent in three places: "contione,

[28] The location of the *curia* in the group is discussed in Marchetti-Longhi, *RendPontAcc*, Ser. III, Vol. XII, 267-279. The favored conjecture at present is to locate it on the border of the Largo Argentina precinct, where an enclosure of suitable size has been discovered. The suggestion that the *curia* was in fact equivalent to the temple of Venus Victrix (which would be extremely attractive in the light of parallels with the Roman *comitium* and the so-called *comitium* and *curia* at Cosa) is highly improbable because of the limited size of the theater temple. The mere existence of the *curia*, however, in some close topographical connection with the theater, does provide one more bit of evidence for the connection of theater and politics and against Marchetti-Longhi's complete denial of political considerations in relation to Pompey's construction.

[29] See above, pp. 14 and 24.

comitiis, ludorum gladiatorumque consessu," and remarks in his letters describe this political expression at the theater.[30]

The tenuousness of the proofs adduced by Marchetti-Longhi for the existence of cult places with theatrical connections in the area before Pompey's time is obvious. He seems often to fall back on "the swampy nature of the site" as one of his capping arguments. By far his most controversial theory is that of the existence of a second, "Italic," temple of Apollo. He specifically identifies this second temple of Apollo with Temple C of the Largo Argentina area and then proposes that the "theatrum et proscaenium ad Apollinis" (Livy xl. 51. 3) be connected with this temple. We have shown the weakness of this theory above,[31] but even if this identification were correct, Marchetti-Longhi's next step would not necessarily follow—i.e., that the "proscaenium et theatrum ad Apollinis" was a direct predecessor of Pompey's theater. A glance at a plan of ancient Rome (Fig. 1) shows that a theater located in front of Temple C would be a considerable distance from Pompey's theater—it would, in fact, be almost as close to the site of the theater of Marcellus—since the gardens and porticoes occupied a space some 200 meters long. But the hypothesis of a second Apollo cult or of various chthonic cults is not necessary to explain or motivate Pompey's theater on religious grounds. That motivation can be found in abundance in the goddess of the theater-temple, Venus Victrix, whose real nature and importance Marchetti-Longhi belittles or passes over.

It is pertinent in this connection to mention not only the general position of importance which Venus held in Roman religion at this period, but also the outstanding significance she held as adopted by Pompey.[32] Allowing for the natural Gallic tendency to give more than her due to "la déesse de l'amour," there is much to be said for Carcopino's statement that during this time philosophy

> . . . is depopulating the traditional Pantheon where only one really living divinity remains: the Venus celebrated by Lucretius, the Venus Felix whose favorite Sulla claimed to be, the Venus Victrix adored by Pompey, the Venus Genetrix from whom Caesar claimed descent, the goddess who consistently represents under all these different names force and pleasure, joy and success.[33]

The near coincidence in date between the probable writing and publication of the proem of the *De Rerum Natura* and the dedication of Pompey's theater-temple is certainly meaningful.[34]

---

[30] *Sest.* 49. 105. In the letters see especially *Att.* ii. 19. 2-3.   [31] See pp. 18-22.

[32] I owe much in the following pages to the brilliant synthesis achieved by Robert Schilling in his monograph, *La religion romaine de Vénus*. I have accepted his general view of the conceptual history of the goddess, but perhaps would grant even more weight than he does to the personal influence of Sulla, Pompey, Caesar, and Augustus.

[33] ". . . dépeuple le panthéon traditionnel où il ne subsiste plus qu'une divinité véritablement vivante: la Vénus qu'a chantée Lucrèce, la Vénus Felix dont Sulla s'est proclamé le favori, la Vénus Victrix qu'adore Pompée, la Vénus Genetrix dont César se prétend issu, la déesse qui sous ces différents vocables n'incarne toujours que la force et la volupté, la joie et le succès." (*César*, p. 600)

[34] This parallel is mentioned by Boyancé ("Lucrèce et son disciple," *REA*, LII [1950], 220),

Venus, starting from a Latin magico-religious concept roughly equivalent to grace, profited immensely from two factors in the second and first centuries B.C.: the stream of Hellenization which brought with it the Greek artistic and literary representations of Aphrodite as goddess of beauty and love and creative force; and, equally important, her adoption as personal protective deity by the political giants of the first century.

The first man so to adapt Venus to the role of personal-political goddess was Sulla.[35] Appian tells of his consulting the Delphic oracle and being commanded to honor the goddess at Aphrodisias in Caria, with votive gifts. The cognomen "Felix" which he assumed became "Epaphroditos" in Greek, and ought to be connected in thought with Venus Felix rather than Felicitas as protective deity. The colony of Sulla's veterans at Pompeii bore the name of Colonia Veneria,[36] and the Venus Physica of Pompeian wall paintings is certainly similar to, though not identical with, the Sullan concept of the goddess.[37] Probably Memmius, since he was a member of Sulla's family, was also a particular devotee of the Sullan Venus, and hence would derive a part of the appropriateness of Lucretius' proem.

Controversy has arisen over the relative accuracy of Tertullian and Tiro in referring to Pompey's goddess. The former calls her merely Venus, the latter merely Victoria.[38] Both are giving an inaccurate or incomplete name to the temple, but their reasons are easily understandable. Two modern Italians might be similarly inaccurate in referring to the church of Santa Maria della Vittoria as merely "Santa Maria" or merely "La Vittoria." Furthermore, Tertullian may have had the motive of wanting to suggest, by omitting the limiting epithet, the amatory domain of the goddess. But Pompey, when he gave her the epithet Victrix in his theater-temple, wanted to emphasize that phase of Venus' activity which pertained to victory, both personal and national. Although there is no definite evidence of the use of the actual epithet in Latin before Pompey's time, it was not as gratuitous as Marchetti-Longhi would lead us to believe: Sulla's *felicitas*—Venus-granted, as he would have it—is personal success or victory. The Etruscan goddess "Turan," who undoubtedly influenced the development of the Roman goddess, is often represented as definitely associated with the concept of personal victory.[39] The feast of the Vinalia, one of the more important

---

who expresses mild astonishment that it has been neglected by literary historians. I find it equally strange that it has, as far as I can discover, been completely ignored by archaeologists writing on this subject.

[35] For a detailed discussion of Sulla's Venus see Schilling, pp. 272-295; Gagé, "La théologie de la Victoire impériale," *RHist*, CLXXI (1933), 36-37; Roscher, *Lexicon der Mythologie*, VI, cols. 192-193; and Lanzani, *Lucio Cornelio Silla Dittatore*, pp. 291-292, 345-366.

[36] Other Sullan colonies which had "Veneria" as part of their titles were Abellinum and Hadria. See Lanzani, pp. 137 and 142, and the references there cited.

[37] Schilling, pp. 287ff. Note especially p. 287, n. 1, where he convincingly refutes the contention of Pais, Gagé, and others that the famous Pompeian wall painting of Venus drawn in a chariot by four elephants must refer to Pompey's triumph of 82 B.C.

[38] *De Spect.* 10. 5; Gell. *NA*, X. 1. 7.

[39] Schilling, pp. 168-173.

festivities of Venus, was mythologically and historically the commemoration of Roman victories gained with the help and through the intercession of the goddess.[40] The cult of Venus Erycina, imported from Sicily at the behest of the Sybilline books to protect the Romans from the Carthaginians, must have emphasized to some extent the ability of the goddess to bring victory, as she had when the Romans took Eryx in 248 B.C. Finally, in this same cult as well as in the later more developed worship of her as *Aeneadum genetrix* by Caesar and others, she was portrayed as progenitor of Rome's founders and, as such, an interested party in the state's fortunes and victories.

Pompey's preoccupation with Venus Victrix and the way in which the worship of the goddess was appropriated by Caesar are both suggested by Plutarch in his account of Pompey's dream on the eve of the battle of Pharsalus:

> During the night Pompey dreamed that he was applauded by the people as he walked into his theater, and that he presented the priest of Venus Victrix with many spoils of war. And he was happy for these things. But on the other hand the vision terrified him, since he feared that reputation and glory might shift from him to the family of Caesar, which went back to Aphrodite.[41]

In fact, Caesar seems to have vowed a temple to Venus Victrix before this battle,[42] and only later changed the appellation of the goddess to Genetrix, a title which was not meant to exclude the connotations of victory, but rather to justify these, and other benefits of the goddess, by emphasizing her family ties with the Roman state on a national plane and the Julian *gens* on a personal plane. Mommsen, in a note on the "ludi Victoriae Caesaris," states "vere *eadem* est Venus victrix et Iuliorum genetrix."[43]

Venus continued to be worshiped under the title Victrix, and this worship spread throughout the Empire. Literary evidence suggests nothing in addition to Pompey's temple,[44] but epigraphical evidence is quite plentiful, especially for the Danube provinces.[45]

[40] *Ibid.*, pp. 93-97.

[41] τῆς δὲ νυκτὸς ἔδοξε κατὰ τοὺς ὕπνους Πομπήιος εἰς τὸ θέατρον εἰσιόντος αὐτοῦ κροτεῖν τὸν δῆμον, αὐτὸς δὲ κοσμεῖν ἱερὸν Ἀφροδίτης νικηφόρου πολλοῖς λαφύροις. καὶ τὰ μὲν ἐθάρρει, τὰ δ'ὑπέθραττεν αὐτὸν ἡ ὄψις, δεδοικότα μὴ τῷ γένει τῷ Καίσαρος εἰς Ἀφροδίτην ἀνήκοντι δόξα καὶ λαμπρότης ἀπ' αὐτοῦ γένηται. (*Vit. Pomp.* 68. 2)

[42] Appian *BC* ii. 68. 281.

[43] *CIL*, I², pp. 322-323: *s.v.* "XIII-III K·AVG, ludi Victoriae Caesaris."

[44] Plin. *HN* xv. 29. 125, "myrto Veneris Victricis coronatus," is the only independent literary reference I have found.

[45] List of dedicatory inscriptions to Venus Victrix in *CIL*:

II	23	(Merobriga, Lusitania)
II	470	(Emerita, Lusitania)
III	1115	(Apulum, Dacia)
III	1797	(Narona, Dalmatia)
III	1964	(Salonae, Dalmatia)
III	1965	(Salonae, Dalmatia)
III	2770	(Riditae, Dalmatia)
III	2805	(Scardona, Dalmatia)

Furthermore, the goddess had a second shrine in Rome itself, located on the Capitoline hill.[46]

In addition to evidence pointing toward a far more important and widespread cult than has usually been assumed, there is some evidence for that "specific" association of the goddess with *ludi scaenici* which Marchetti-Longhi demands. First, as partaking of the nature of the goddess "Victoria," Pompey's deity asssuredly fits in the middle of a series of three such victory goddesses, two of whom were honored by regular annual *ludi*. In the face of the calendar notations of the *ludi Victoriae Sullanae* (October 26-November 1) and the *ludi Victoriae Caesaris* (July 20-30), how is it possible to maintain that Venus Victrix is not a suitable divinity for the offering of *ludi*?[47] Second, Venus herself shows other signs of being at home in the theater. An inscription from Spain speaks of "signa Veneris Genetricis et Cupidinis ad theatrum."[48] Livy (xxx. 38. 10) mentions that when the *ludi Apollinares* could not be held at their regular place in the year 202 B.C. because of floods, they were transferred "ad aedem Veneris Erucinae extra portam Collinam." Mommsen's list of *ludi* established during the Imperial period includes one day, April 1, dedicated to Venus,[49] while the Lex Coloniae Genetivae stipulates that the aediles, in addition to providing three days of games to the Capitoline triad, shall also give one day's games in honor of Venus, "in circo aut in foro."[50]

Four other shrine existed in Pompey's theater, according to the *Fasti Amiterni* and *Alliferni*. The divinities of three are known: Honos, Virtus, and Felicitas. The fourth has frustrated conjecture.[51] The presence of Felicitas here gives further evi-

---

III	3160	(loc. incert. Dalmatia)
III	4152	(Savaria, Pannonia Sup.)
III	4167	(Savaria, Pannonia Sup.)
III	7663	(Napoca, Dacia)
III	11139	(Carnuntum, Pannonia Sup.)
III	11140	(Carnuntum, Pannonia Sup.)
V	2805	(Patavium, Gallia Cis.)
V	8249	(Aquileia, Gallia Cis.) Doubtful; depends on restoration of abbreviation "V" in broken space before "VICTRICI."
VI	785	(Rome, "post aedem D. Mariae cognomento in Cripta," i.e., in the area of Pompey's theater.
VIII	14809	(Schauwasch, Africa Proconsularis)
X	7013	(Hybla Maior, Sicilia)
XI	5928	(Tifernum Tiberinum, Umbria)

[46] She may have shared this shrine with two other divinities. The calendar notices (*Fast. Amit. Arv.* ad vii Id. Oct., *CIL*, I², pp. 214, 245, 331) have "Genio Publico, Faustae Felicitati, Veneri Victrici in Capitolio." Roscher (*Lexicon der Mythologie*, VI, col. 199) relates the reference to Venus shrines in Suetonius *Caligula* 7 and *Galba* 18.2, to this Capitoline shrine of Venus Victrix.

[47] See the list of *ludi* by Mommsen, *CIL*, I², pp. 299-301.

[48] *CIL*, II, 3270, from Castulo, modern Cazlona.

[49] *CIL*, I², p. 301.

[50] *CIL*, II, 5439, section 71. Mommsen states (*EphEp*, III, 102) that these games are in imitation of the games instituted by Caesar and called either "ludi Victoriae Caesaris" or "ludi Veneris." From this he draws support for Hirschfeld's conjecture that the colony took its name from the Julian divinity, Venus "genetrix."

[51] *CIL*, I², p. 324, ad PRID · ID · AVG: "Veneri victrici, Hon (ori), Virt (uti), Felicitati in theatro

dence for the importance which Pompey attached to his inheritance from Sulla. For the architectural arrangement of the four shrines there is no direct evidence, but one may make a strong conjecture on the basis of a heretofore unnoticed parallel, the theater at Herculaneum.[52] The shrines were probably at or near the top of the *cavea* and arranged symmetrically in relation to the central aisle, being themselves located on the line of other aisles. This would also tally with Suetonius' description of Claudius' sacrifice "apud superiores aedes."[53]

The enticing question raised by Plutarch's mention of the theater at Mytilene as a model for Pompey's theater must remain without a definite answer. Unfortunately, there exist neither remains nor descriptions of this Lesbian theater sufficient to give evidence of architectural idiosyncrasies—or the lack of them—which could amplify the meaning of Plutarch's statement.[54] The lack of any parallel among known Greek theaters, however, should lead one to be extremely dubious of Caputo's contention, however attractive it might be, that Pompey got from Mytilene the idea for the temple at the top of his theater; he suggests that the sanctuary within which the Greek theater was "ordinarily included" had the temple placed above the *cavea* at Mytilene.[55]

Another circumstance should here be discussed, however, which may suggest an explanation for the fact, if not the form, of Pompey's borrowing. One of the main parts of the Pompeian group is the portico behind the theater, an immense rectangular enclosure (180 by 135 meters) surrounded by a colonnade, divided into five aisles along its length by free-standing pillars or rows of trees, and provided with an elaborate series of exedras around its circumference (Fig. 19).[56] It is the first public park in Rome, and, according to Grimal in *Les jardins romains*, it does not follow the "naturalistic" Italian tradition of gardens but is an importation of the Hellenistic monumental garden.[57] As such, the Pompeian *porticus* has many descendants in the city of Rome,

---

marmoreo" AMIT. "V(eneri) V(ictrici), H(onori) V(irtuti), V(. . . . . .), Felicita(ti) in theatro Pompei" ALLIF. Mommsen remarks "Tertia V in Allifano quid significet non liquet." Valentia, which Mommsen himself had earlier suggested, he here rejects because this goddess is included in Tertullian's list (*Apol.* 24) of Italian divinities not honored in the city of Rome. But Valetudo is a possibility. It would fit well with the other abstractions honored in the theater and, though infrequent, shows several occurrences: an invocation in the prayer of the Marsi (*CIL*, I², 390-391), a cult presided over by *novemviri* in Mevania (Umbria), altars at Forum Sempronii (Umbria) and Aquileia, dedications at Noricum and Carnuntum, and a temple in Mauretania. Most pertinent is her appearance on a coin of M' Acilius minted in 54 B.C. (Grueber, *Coins of Rom. Rep. in Brit. Mus.*, I, 496). For further details and references consult Weinstock in *RE*, VIII A, cols. 264-270, s.v. "Valetudo."

[52] See below, pp. 74-75.   [53] *Claud.* 21. 1.

[54] See R. Koldewey, *Die antiken Bauten der Insel Lesbos*, pp. 8-9; *AA*, XLIII (1928), 620; R. Herbst in *RE*, XVI, col. 1418, s.v. "Mytilene."

[55] *Dioniso*, XVII, 176. On the other hand, one may not categorically deny this possibility or ignore it, as Rumpf and Marchetti-Longhi have done. A topographical collocation of theater and temple, even if they were as far removed from one another as the Parthenon and theater of Dionysos in Athens, might have helped to call the combined temple-theater form to Pompey's mind.

[56] See Platner-Ashby, s.v. "Porticus Pompei"; Marchetti-Longhi, *RendPontAcc*, Ser. III, Vol. XII, 260-267, with figs. 9-10.

[57] Pp. 183-188.

e.g., the Porticus Liviae (Fig. 20), the Porticus Divorum, the Isaeum.[58] It has been suggested that such gardens have strong religious associations in their origins, and in the Greek world they were frequently part of the *heroa* or cult places of immortalized humans.[59] There is some evidence that a shrine was sometimes placed in the center of a Hellenistic garden, and Grimal draws the parallel between this and the small temple of Concord in the center of the Porticus Liviae.[60] On the other hand, such porticoes seem also to belong to another special architectural tradition, an Alexandrian —perhaps more broadly Hellenistic—ruler cult sanctuary adopted by Caesar in the Kaisareia at Alexandria and Antioch.[61] The evidence for the prototypes of this Imperial sanctuary has been collected and discussed by Erik Sjöqvist, and he has further shown the extensive adoption of the scheme at the hands of the Julio-Claudian emperors in connection with their gradual introduction of the symbolism of the ruler cult into Rome, deriving the Saepta Julia, Porticus Liviae, Porticus Divorum, and Templum Divi Claudii, as well as some of the features of the Imperial fora, from the Kaisareion and its Hellenistic models.[62]

There is no evidence for a shrine within the *porticus* of Pompey; in other respects it is highly suggestive of the Kaisareion form. It may even be said to contain a central "processional way" emphasized by the line of the *aula regia* of the theater stage building and perhaps even bridged by arches, according to the generally accepted interpretation of its representation on the Severan marble map.[63] Obviously this derivation, if valid, could not be spelled out for the Romans, to whom regal pomp was suspect, just as the personal and political significance of Venus Victrix could not be spelled out. Returning to Plutarch's account of Pompey's stay at Mytilene, one observes that the ceremonies that Pompey witnessed in the theater which he liked so much were in fact a glorification of his own deeds.[64] As stated above, there is some evidence that the Hellenistic ruler cult was sometimes associated with the theater building and its surroundings.[65] It is easy to suppose that Pompey may have observed this in his travels in the East in general and that the personal adulation which he received in Mytilene where he was welcomed as liberator of the city may have brought home to him the value of a theater building and its surroundings for personal propaganda of a sort approaching—if distantly—the ultimate deification of the Roman *princeps*. Much the same idea is expressed in the shrine to Venus Victrix as in the temple of Venus Gene-

---

[58] Pierre Grimal, *Les jardins romains*, pp. 188-191, 197-198. For the Porticus Divorum see Platner-Ashby, *s.v.* "Divorum templum."

[59] Grimal, pp. 76-82, 328-335.

[60] *Ibid.*, p. 189.

[61] See Erik Sjöqvist, "Kaisareion, a Study in Architectural Iconography," *Opuscula Romana*, I (1954), 86-95.

[62] *Ibid.*, pp. 95-108.

[63] See Marchetti-Longhi, *RendPontAcc*, Ser. III, Vol. XII, 260-262. They were perhaps constructed only later under Augustus. Marchetti-Longhi describes the middle of the *quadriporticus* as a "grande viale facente capo al giano medesimo" (p. 262).

[64] *Vit. Pomp.* 42. 4, ὑπόθεσιν μίαν ἔχοντα τὰς ἐκείνου πράξεις.

[65] Chap. II, n. 40.

trix in the Forum Julium, and possibly much the same idea is expressed in the *porticus* and *hecatostylon* as in the *porticus post scaenam* at Leptis Magna with its temple to the Divi Augusti.[66] In both cases the meaning in Pompey's structure is less explicit. Later examples of religious adjuncts to the Roman theater building will show several instances involving the Imperial cult directly or indirectly, and just as the form of the *cavea* shrine seems to go back to the theater of Pompey, so does the notion of its use for religio-political glorification. It may be suggested that this notion, rather than any architectural detail, is the most significant borrowing from Mytilene.

Neither the idea of theatrical performances in front of a temple nor the architectural pattern of temple steps serving as a semicircular *theatron* came, insofar as one can determine, from the Hellenistic world, but both, it has been shown, were present in relative abundance in the Italo-Roman world, to serve as a model for Pompey's architect. Architecturally, despite Pompey's assertion that he was dedicating principally a temple, the theater was now the dominant element, as it was to be to an even greater extent in the later examples of the same combination.

[66] See below, p. 95.

CHAPTER IV
IMPERIAL THEATER BUILDINGS COMBINED WITH TEMPLES

"commemorabimus . . . loca, quibus praesidibus dicentur." (Tert. *De Spect.* 4. 4)

IMPERIAL THEATER BUILDINGS
COMBINED WITH TEMPLES

ONCE ESTABLISHED, the Roman combination of theater and temple did not die out with the construction of Pompey's edifice in the Campus Martius. Many examples of both *cavea* shrines and other patterns of collocation are to be found throughout Italy and the various provinces of the Empire, and it is the purpose of this chapter to point out and describe as many of these as have not been completely obliterated by time, poor excavation, or insufficient publication.

The thorough publication in recent years of two such shrines, at Leptis Magna and at Vienne, should serve to call the archaeologist's attention to parallel architectural features in theaters which were either published long ago or, because their ruins have long been visible, have never been deemed worthy of a good descriptive publication. Since the very top of the superstructure of a theater would be earliest and most susceptible to ruin, the archaeological indications of the existence of such a *sacellum* at the top of a theater *cavea* would not be immediately obvious. The only signs might be a change in the weight, spacing, or direction of the radial walls of the auditorium substructure at the point where the shrine stood. Consequently the possibility of either affirming or denying the existence of shrines in many Roman theaters—perhaps the majority—has been irrevocably lost.[1] In the examples which follow, only those theaters are cited for which the likely existence of a shrine has been recognized, or which are so closely parallel in form to these as to demand the recognition of the probable presence of a shrine.

The theaters of the African provinces are here treated as a group because of the relatively high frequency of sure examples of temples among them and because of certain unique factors which may enter into the interpretation of their occurrence here.

The best documented of the theater-temples is at Leptis Magna in Tripolitania. The theater has not been completely published, but the parts pertinent to this study have been fully described in an article on the theater's architectural peculiarities by the Italian archaeologist, Giacomo Caputo.[2] A small, shallow temple stands at the top of the theater *cavea* on the central axis (Fig. 22). Its platform is on the same level as that of the portico which encircles the *cavea* and extends forward several feet to accommodate the temple. There is no *pronaos*, but a six-column porch is placed directly in front of the *cella*, with two additional columns behind in the *cella* entrance. The back wall of the *cella* coincides with the back wall of the *cavea* and is consequently slightly

---

[1] Cf. Frézouls, "Teatri romani dell'Africa francese," *Dioniso*, xv (1952), 100. "A Khamissa o a Bône, per esempio, non si può sapere se ci fosse un tempietto o meno."

[2] "Architettura del teatro di Leptis Magna," *Dioniso*, xiii (1950), 164-178. The description of the remains of the temple is found pp. 169-174, with plans, figs. 1-3. See also for the theater as a whole *AA*, lv (1940), cols. 551-552, and lvi (1941), cols. 716-724.

curved. Enough of the columns and trabeation has been found to establish the height of the temple above the floor level of the portico as approximately twelve meters, enough to dominate the portico itself, which is constructed of smaller columns. The dedicatory inscription from the architrave of the temple is extant: CERERI AVGVSTAE SACRVM/ C · RVBELLIVS · BLANDVS · COS · PONT · PRO · COS · DEDIC · SVPHVNIBAL · ORNA-TRIX · PA[TRIAE] · ANNOBALIS · RVSONIS [F.D.] S.P.F.C.[3] From another inscription on the arch of Tiberius in the same city the date of Rubellius' proconsulship is established as A.D. 35/6. The construction of the theater itself dates from the year A.D. 1/2.[4] How-ever, it is almost certain that the temple was planned as part of the original Augustan project because of the existence in the first structure of a wide staircase approaching the shrine from the rear and sides. In the Severan period new columns of granite and cipollino were substituted for the original limestone ones. A confirmation of the identity of the divinity of the temple is found in the cult statue which stood on the pre-served base at the back of the *cella* (Fig. 21).[5] It is of a heavy, but quite gracefully carved female figure with a turreted crown on her head and her right arm bent in a position which suggests that she held a cornucopia. This is a common Ceres type. We know that Ceres was a popular goddess in North Africa, and that she was assimilated to the Phoe-nician goddess Tanit.[6] Furthermore, the only other *cavea* temple in North Africa where one can be certain of the divinity involved, at Dugga, is also dedicated to her.[7] It is pos-sible that the woman with the Punic name, Suphunibal, who is called here and else-where in Leptis *ornatrix patriae*, was a priestess of Ceres Augusta. The additional appel-lation of the goddess as "Augusta" serves merely to accentuate the close bond with the Imperial cult which is emphasized in so many public works throughout the provinces, and which is so strongly brought out at Leptis Magna through the temple behind the stage building.[8]

A recent careful restudy of the Roman theater at Tipasa in Algeria, late second or early third century A.D. in date, has clearly demonstrated the probability of the existence of a similar *cavea* shrine at this site.[9] It would not be without profit to describe the evidence in some detail here, since the acuteness with which M. Frézouls deduced the presence of a shrine in this theater seems to provide the best hints for the exam-ination of new sites and the re-examination of old sites with a view to confirming or denying the presence of similar religious architectural features. The substructures of the theater at Tipasa—like those of almost all Roman theaters, including most of those built with the partial utilization of the natural slope of a hillside but needing

---

[3] Caputo, *Dioniso*, XIII, 165.   [4] *AA*, LVI (1941), col. 717.

[5] Described by Caputo, *Dioniso*, XIII, 174-176, with photographs, figs. 4-6.

[6] Gilbert Charles-Picard, *Les religions de l'Afrique antique*, p. 87.

[7] See below, p. 61.   [8] See below, p. 95.

[9] Edmond Frézouls, "Le théâtre romain de Tipasa," *MélRome*, LXIV (1952), 111-177, with a succinct discussion of the problem of the shrine in "Teatri romani dell'Africa francese," *Dioniso*, XV (1952), 99-101. Until the last decade the ruins were in very bad condition, and re-ceived only a short paragraph in Stéphane Gsell's extensive "Tipasa," *MélRome*, XIV (1894), 291-450: "Les ruines . . . en fort mauvais état" (p. 355).

constructional support near the top—determine a series of radiating vaulted chambers (Fig. 23). The top vaults naturally slope in accordance with the angle of incline of the *cavea*. However, one of these, the central vault in the circumference of the *cavea*, is horizontal where it is preserved, and is on a somewhat lower level than the others. The difference cannot be explained in terms of the vaulted chamber below; i.e., it cannot be interpreted solely as suggesting a special entrance on the central axis of the theater, an interpretation which has often been proposed for other theaters to explain, or explain away, peculiarities of construction at this point in the *cavea*.[10] In fact, the horizontal central vault must show itself in the superstructure as a level platform of approximately one sector's width in the middle of the top rows of the auditorium, precisely the kind of platform on which rest the small temple at Leptis Magna and others described below. The depth of the temple would be between four and five meters, and the width, though limited to a maximum of four and a half meters, would still be somewhat larger than that of the *cavea* shrine at Calama.[11] Frézouls proposes a proportionate height which would raise the top of the temple to the level of the top of the back wall of the *cavea*.[12]

The ruins of the theater at Dugga also present architectural peculiarities at the center of the back of the *cavea* (Fig. 24).[13] Two heavy parallel walls extend out beyond the circumference of the auditorium at this point. Inside the theater was found the following inscription: CERERI AVG SACRVM / M LICINIVS M L TYRANNVS ET LICINIA PRISCA / VOTO SVSCEPTO PRO [SA]LVTE M LICINI PATRONI / CELLAM CVM PORTICIBV [S . . . . . . P] OSVERVNT.[14] Carton, in the main publication of the theater, asks: "Où était le sanctuaire, sans doute une chapelle prostyle, dont il est question ici, dans le théâtre ou en dehors de lui?"[15] He calls the structure at the back of the *cavea* "la porte centrale, flanquée de deux contreforts."[16] But it is now most probable, in the light of the parallel furnished by the theater at Leptis Magna, that these "buttresses" are in fact the supporting walls for a *cavea* shrine dedicated to Ceres Augusta. The center aisle of the theater, as seen both from photographs and from reconstructions,[17] is an especially dominating feature architecturally and seems to lead the eye up to the position of the little temple as well as to provide a monumental approach.[18] Although appar-

[10] E.g., the theaters at Dugga (see next paragraph) and at Nicopolis (see below, p. 71, n. 63).
[11] See below, p. 62. [12] *MélRome*, LXIV, 142.
[13] The theater was extensively published by Carton, "Le théâtre romain de Dugga," *Mémoirs présentés par divers savants à l'Académie*, XI (1902), 70-191. See the general plan, pl. II.
[14] Text *ibid.*, p. 122, n. 12. The last line is completed by Caputo ("Teatri romani d'Africa," *Dioniso*, X [1947], 16) as follows: "cellam cum porticibu[s et statua p]osuerunt."
[15] *Mémoirs présentés par divers savants à l'Académie*, XI, 122, n. 12.
[16] *Ibid.*, p. 96.
[17] Note especially the photograph in Carton, pl. XIII. An architect's reconstruction is found in Homer F. Pfeiffer, "The Ancient Roman Theater at Dugga," *MAAR*, IX (1931), 145-156 and plates 11-15. The restored drawing (plate 11) shows a back staircase on the axis of the *cavea*, with projecting walls, but the same drawing also shows clearly the dominating central stairway within the *cavea*.
[18] This serves to emphasize the axiality of the whole monument, a typically and strongly

ently no trace of permanent stairs has been found behind the *cavea*, it is possible that the shrine was also approachable from the rear or sides, as at Leptis Magna. Also, if Caputo correctly interprets "cum porticibus" as referring to an amphiprostyle temple,[19] the shrine of Ceres may have had the unusual feature of a porch at the back, overhanging the exterior of the theater. This latter element would certainly have called for a staircase approaching from the rear. In view of the tenuousness of the evidence and the present lack of parallels, it seems best to hold Caputo's hypothesis in abeyance and view the Dugga theater-temple as a typical prostyle shrine like those that can be observed in other Roman theaters.[20]

The theater at Guelma, ancient Calama, constructed near the beginning of the third century A.D., contains a quite well-preserved example of a *cavea* shrine (Fig. 25).[21] The comparatively small auditorium is built on a natural slope and the wall encircling the top of the *cavea* is pierced by four entrances, two of which immediately flank the little temple, which projects slightly beyond the circumference wall. There is no visible sign of a porch, just as there was apparently no portico surmounting the *cavea* as a whole,[22] but the shrine is a simple rectangular chamber approximately four meters wide and four and a half meters deep. Its most interesting feature is a semicircular apse at the rear, which must have contained the cult statue. It is not possible to identify the divinity.[23]

There are also indications of a temple in the theater at Philippeville, ancient Rusicade, which was constructed shortly after the reign of Hadrian (Fig. 26).[24] Here the lower half of the auditorium, of moderate size, is laid on the natural slope while the upper portion rises on vaulted substructures. Behind the one row of vaulted cham-

---

Roman feature. This has been noted above in discussing the Republican sanctuaries in Latium. Cf. Frézoul's remark on the theater at Tipasa: "Le même souci de faire un tout complet et équilibré apparaît avec la présence du *sacellum*, qui, outre sa valeur religieuse, souligne vigoureusement, face à la *valva regia* et à la niche plus large du pulpitum, l'axe nord-sud du théâtre. Le même sens de la simplicité et de l'économie se laisse deviner, selon notre hypothèse, dans le recul de la *praecinctio* centrale jusque vers l'entrée du sanctuaire, auquel elle donnerait ainsi accès." (*MélRome*, LXIV, 173.)

[19] *Dioniso*, x, 16 and n. 6.

[20] Frézouls (*MélRome*, LXIV, 140-141, n. 5), in citing likely parallels to the Tipasa shrine, says that at Dugga and at Timgad "la chose est également possible; nous n'osons pourtant être aussi affirmatif que M. G. Caputo." However, in the general article which he wrote slightly later, he is more positive. (*Dioniso*, xv, 100)

[21] See Stéphane Gsell, *Les monuments antiques de l'Algérie*, pp. 194-197 with plan, fig. 64. An earlier reconstructed plan is given by Wieseler, *Theatergebäude*, p. 110, Supplementtafel A, 21 (after Ravoisié, *Exploration scientifique de l'Algérie*, Paris, 1846, II, pl. 30. fig. 1). In his restored drawing, Ravoisié showed a seated statue on the base at the rear of the shrine. See also Caputo, *Dioniso*, x, 11.

[22] Ravoisié, however, reconstructs a portico; see Wieseler, p. 110.

[23] The patroness at whose expense the theater was constructed, Annia Aelia Restituta, was a *flaminica Augustorum* (*CIL*, VIII, 5365, 5366). This might suggest again a connection with the Imperial cult.

[24] Described in Gsell, *Les monuments antiques de l'Algérie*, pp. 192-194, with plan, fig. 63. Brief description in Caputo, *Dioniso*, x, 12.

bers lies an unroofed corridor giving access to the seats of the *cavea* by means of staircases at intervals. This corridor is interrupted in the middle, however, by two nearly parallel heavy foundation walls which extend outward beyond the back wall of the corridor and inward into the *cavea* for nearly four meters. These are connected by a crosswall at the front, and by a second wall some five meters behind the front, which probably represents a divisional wall in the shrine above between *cella* and *pronaos*. There seem to be no indications of a porch, though the platform provided by the *cavea* substructures into which the temple foundation projects would be sufficiently large to allow a row of columns along the front. The width of the main platform at the front is about six meters, increasing to seven at the rear. Just as at Calama, two of the entrances into the outside corridor, with their corresponding staircases leading up through the substructures to the *praecinctio* in front of the *summum maenianum*, directly flank the shrine.

At Timgad, the interpretation of the remains of the theater is not as clear as at those sites previously discussed (Fig. 27).[25] The top portions of the structure are described as being in extremely ruined condition.[26] The plans, however, show a rectangular construction, wider than it is deep, projecting from the back of the center of the *cavea*. Its walls apparently do not extend into the circumference of the auditorium itself. Interpreted as an entrance because of indications of a wide door piercing it at the back and front, and a narrow opening at each side,[27] it may well have served this purpose if the plans are correct in showing no other entrances along the rear into the portico surmounting the *cavea*. But even if it functioned as a monumental and roofed back entrance, it may at the same time have been the foundation of a platform for a small shrine since the openings indicated in the side walls are not sufficiently large to have weakened them measurably and the front wall is in fact proportionately very heavy. On the other hand, since the original excavators postulated an entrance at this point, it seems quite possible, in view of the scanty nature of the remains, that they interpreted as doors what were only breaks in the walls caused by the process of ruin. In this case, the walls would be the actual walls of a small shrine (about six meters in width) which lay behind the portico on the central axis of the theater. There is no certain indication as to what divinity would have been honored in the temple, but there is a dedicatory inscription which establishes a connection with the theater, in some capacity, for Ceres Augusta,[28] the goddess honored in the Dugga and Leptis

---

[25] See Boeswillwald, Cagnat, and Ballu, *Timgad*, pp. 93-120; Courtois, *Timgad, Antique Thamugadi*, pp. 34-38; Gsell, *Les monuments antiques de l'Algérie*, pp. 197-199; all with plans.

[26] Of the second *maenianum*, Boeswillwald states, "Il ne reste, pour ainsi dire, pas une pierre de cette partie du théâtre"; and of the third, "Toute cette partie est aujourd'hui extrêmement ruinée et c'est par l'imagination seule et la comparaison avec d'autres théâtres que l'on peut s'en faire une idée." (*Timgad*, pp. 96-97.)

[27] "Une entrée spéciale, ménagée au milieu de la courbe, qui est représentée aujourd'hui par un quadrilatère percé de deux ouvertures latérales." (Boeswillwald *et al.*, Timgad, p. 97) Gsell and Courtois do not even mention this element. Caputo accepts it as a *sacellum* without comment (*Dioniso*, x, 19, and xiii, 171), while Frézouls expresses some hesitation (see above, n. 20).

[28] See Caputo, *Dioniso*, x, 19.

Magna theaters. The Timgad theater was constructed during the period of the Antonines.

The last of the North African theaters for which there is good evidence of a *cavea* temple is at Cherchel, ancient Caesarea in Mauretania (Fig. 28).[29] Here the theater, whose orchestra was turned into an amphitheatrical arena in the late Empire, was surmounted by a portico, and at the midpoint and extending somewhat behind the portico there exist the foundations for a rectangular construction six meters wide and nearly five meters deep. There are two flights of steps entering the portico from the rear near this foundation, and though none of the superstructure above the platform remains, one is led strongly to hypothesize the existence of another theater sanctuary similar to the six described above. The construction of this theater has been attributed to the reign of the puppet prince Juba II. If this is correct it would be the earliest of the structures here discussed.[30]

In the area of North Africa as a whole, the frequency of occurrence of the *cavea* shrine is very high. Of those theaters for which the present state of excavation and publication might reasonably be expected to produce evidence for such shrines if they had existed, more than half have yielded up such evidence. Those which have not are the theaters at Djemila (Cuicul), Schemtou (Simitthu), Carthage, Sabratha, and Apollonia. About the rest it seems impossible to make any statement, either negative or positive, without further excavation or exploration.[31]

Are there any factors which might explain this relative frequency of the theater-temple in North Africa? Two explanations come to mind, neither of which is meant sufficiently to explain the existence of the form itself, but both of which throw some light on its popularity in this region of the Empire.

When Juba II was placed in the kingship of Mauretania in 25 B.C., he set out to introduce elements of Greco-Roman culture to his subjects, building Caesarea as his capital and the focal point for this civilizing process. When the kingdom was trans-

[29] Described by Stéphane Gsell, *Cherchel*, pp. 104-108, with plan.

[30] Gsell's dating is based on the style of the architectural decoration, which "indique une excellente époque," and the feeling that Caesarea under Juba would have been likely to possess a theater (*Cherchel*, p. 107). These criteria seem vague, but the attribution is given more weight with its acceptance by Frézouls, based, in all probability, on a recent re-examination. (See *Dioniso*, xv, 100-101.)

[31] The general statements in this paragraph are founded on a list of theaters of the North African provinces by F. Drexel in Friedländer, *Darstellungen aus der Sittengeschichte Roms*, iv, 255-257, completed with modern bibliography, principally *Archäologischer Anzeiger* and *Fasti Archaeologici*. In general, publication of extant monuments is scanty, with details and careful dimensions reserved, when existent, for the personal notebooks of the excavator. But North Africa is still greatly superior to other Mediterranean areas in this respect. Semipopular but scientific descriptions of most sites have been published through the Service des Antiquités of Algeria, and the Direction d'Antiquités et Arts of Tunisia has promoted considerable, though less systematic, publication. For Cyrenaica and Tripolitania much was made available through the short-lived periodical *Africa italiana*. Although the available material is far from complete, it is still possible—and this is the only area in the western Empire where it is now possible—to obtain something approaching an exhaustive, over-all view.

formed into a province, it remained its most important city and as an important sea-port it must have exerted considerable influence on North Africa as a whole.[32] In building the theater of this city, Juba could easily have been influenced by features of the theater of Pompey, which he must have attended many times during the nearly twenty years of his stay in Rome when it was the only theater building in the city. The small shrine at the top of the theater at Cherchel may be a reflection of this influence, and it would be quite natural for the neighboring city of Tipasa, at least, to imitate the capital city of the province in this feature as well as in others.[33]

Another factor which needs to be considered in discussing the theater-temple in Africa is a type of Syrian-Phoenician sanctuary which played at least an occasional part in the religious customs of the natives. Apparently an important feature in the worship of some of the Syrian divinities was a cult ceremony or spectacle witnessed by devotees who stood or sat in rows near the presentation.[34] A small theater was often constructed near the temple and within the sanctuary area to regularize or monumentalize the watching of this ritualistic spectacle.[35] The forms of these *theatra* are somewhat diverse.

[32] See the historical introduction in Gsell, *Cherchel*, pp. 9-29.

[33] Frézouls makes the same suggestion (*MélRome*, LXIV, 142) ". . . nous aurions à Tipasa, par une filiation assez attachante, un modeste reflet de l'ouvrage qui dut retenir durant ses années romaines les regards de Juba et inspirer ensuite ses plans."

[34] The nature of these ceremonies is difficult to specify. Lucian (*De Dea Syria* 47-49) speaks of two main festivals celebrated in the court of the temple at Hieropolis, the "descent to the lake" (εἰς τὴν λίμνην κατάβασις) and the "pyre" (πυρή, λαμπάς). The former consisted principally of a procession ending in the sacred bath of the statue of the goddess. In this connection should be mentioned a basin found in the court of the sanctuary of Artemis at Dura (*Excav. Dura, Rep.* III, p. 8). There are other examples of theaters found in connection with an artificial lake: at Jerash was discovered a huge tank bordered by a colonnaded terrace with a theater beyond, and a late Greek inscription from A.D. 535 proves that the complex was used for the feast of Maiumas: "ritualistic submersion of naked women in the presence of an audience seated in a theater." (Rostovtzeff, *Caravan Cities*, pp. 83-84) Frézouls sees similar religious connection with waters in the tiny odeon-type theater at El Hammé ("Les théâtres romains de Syrie," *Annales arch. de Syrie,* II [1952], 79-81). Common both to this festival and the "pyre" was a procession of divine statues, and this may have formed in or passed through the courts which served as "stages" for the theaters. In the "pronaos" type theater of the Dura sanctuaries discussed below, visibility from the seats would have been limited to the small area within the room, and perhaps Cumont is right here when he sees the spectacle as rather "l'exécution de danses et de chants sacrés au son des instruments," although his support for this on the basis of a formal parallel with the Greco-Roman *odeon* does not seem apt in the light of the completely different cultural setting (*Fouilles de Doura-Europos,* p. 202). Charles-Picard (*Les religions de l'Afrique antique,* p. 161) speaks of "de véritables drames liturgiques" in connection with the Dugga sanctuary. Instructive in any effort to reconstruct these ceremonies are the discoveries of two foundations in the court at Delos, just below the theater of the Syrian sanctuary; with the aid of inscriptions these have been identified as the base for a throne of the goddess and the base of an altar. (Cf. Will, "Le sanctuaire syrien de Délos," *Annales arch. de Syrie,* I [1951], 78, and notes.) He comments, "A certaines fêtes qui reunissaient les fidèles dans le théâtre, on transportait l'idole de la déesse de son naos de la Cour sur le trône de la Terrasse: à la foule assemblée sur les gradins de la cavea la déesse apparaissait dans toute sa splendeur dans l'ouverture de l'orchestre, tout comme son épiphanie pouvait se placer à Doura dans la porte menant de la 'salle aux gradins' à sa chapelle."

[35] "Le théâtre est une solution architecturale possible, mais nullement obligatoire dans un sanctuaire syrien. A Délos, c'est sans doute la foule des croyants et aussi le désir de donner un aspect monumental au sanctuaire qui explique son édification." (Will, *Annales arch. de Syrie,* I,

At Dura five such small auditoriums have been found, attached to the temples of Atargatis, Artemis Nannaia (Fig. 29), Artemis Azzanathkona, Adonis and Gaddé.[36] Rostovtzeff describes the type as follows: "It is a small hall before the Holy of Holies with steps on both of its longer sides, a kind of tiny theater. The seats in this theater were the private property of definite people, in the same way as are particular pews in Catholic and Protestant churches today."[37] Hopkins refers to "theatre-like *pronaoi*."[38] In one instance, the shrine of Artemis Nannaia, the small rectangular hall with rows of seats was later replaced by a somewhat larger odeon-like structure at the side of the sacred area opposite the *naos*. Another form may be seen in the hypaethral temple at Seleucia-on-the-Tigris (Fig. 30), which has a small semicircular theater facing directly onto the outer court at the center of one side,[39] making this sanctuary roughly parallel to the later form of the Nannaia sanctuary at Dura. Of the same general type are three theater-temple combinations in the Houran: at Sur, at Sahr, and the temple of Baal Shamin at Si'.[40] At Si' the "theater" consists merely of three steps facing into the temple court, but a Nabatean inscription (dated 33-31 B.C.) speaks of the three parts of the sanctuary as an internal temple, an external temple, and a "Theater."[41]

The disposition of the parts of the two forms of sanctuary described above is characterized by Will as follows:

It is clear that these rooms [the first or "Dura" type] must have permitted the faithful to watch under the best possible conditions the ceremonies conducted in front of the door of the chapel itself where the image of the divinity stood. A closer examination shows that the disposition of Si', Sur, and Sahr is practically the same: the theater [more accurately, the orchestra or stage] is formed by the courtyard which extends in front of the temple itself. The difference is in the scale of the monuments and in their architecture.[42]

---

77) From Lucian's descriptions in *De Dea Syria*, there seems to have been no theater-like construction at Hieropolis. Interestingly, Herodian (v. 5. 9), in describing a sacrifice held by Heliogabalus in Rome, said that the official spectators stood around in a theater-like pattern: περιεστήκει δὲ πᾶσα ἡ σύγκλητος καὶ τὸ ἱππικὸν τάγμα ἐν θεάτρου σχήματι.

[36] The sanctuary of Artemis Nannaia is fully described and discussed in Cumont, *Fouilles de Doura-Europos*, pp. 169-204. For Atargatis: *Excav. Dura, Rep.* III, pp. 9-11, pls. III-IV; for Azzanathkona: *ibid., Rep.* V, pp. 132, 170-200, pls. III, XXIV, XXV; for Adonis: *ibid., Rep.* VII-VIII, p. 145, figs. 39, 43; for Gaddé: *ibid.*, p. 252, fig. 67.

[37] *Caravan Cities*, p. 179.

[38] Clark Hopkins, "The Parthian Temple," *Berytus*, VII (1942), 18.

[39] Briefly mentioned by Hopkins (*Berytus*, VII, 5 and appendix, pp. 17-18). Professor Hopkins has kindly allowed me to examine both a plan and a photograph of this unpublished sanctuary. In the article cited above he mentions the possibility, discussing these temple-theaters in general, that "there may be two original types, one Syrian belonging to the temple proper of certain goddesses, one Iranian and associated only with the court and the district outside the naos" (p. 18). The two probably become blended, however. See the discussion of the Delos sanctuary below.

[40] For Sur: Butler, *Princeton Arch. Exped. Syria*, II A, p. 429, fig. 371; for Sahr: *ibid.* pp. 441-443, fig. 387, and Frézouls, *Annales arch. de Syrie*, II, 81-82; for Si': Butler, *Princeton Arch. Exped. Syria*, II A, pp. 379-380, figs. 324, 329.

[41] Littmann, *Princeton Arch. Exped. Syria*, IV A, p. 77, no. 100 (cited in Frézouls, *Annales arch. de Syrie*, II, 48, n. 6).

[42] "Il est clair que ces salles devaient permettre aux fidèles de voir, dans les meilleurs con-

On a considerably larger and more monumental scale the same disposition is found in the sanctuary of the Dei Siriaci on Delos (Fig. 31), constructed at the end of the second century B.C.[43] Here the auditorium faces directly onto the long side of a long and narrow paved court, at one end of which is the main chapel area. Opposite the theater is a single colonnade, a feature which must have given a stage-like illusion to the court. The theater is bounded on the rear and sides by a rectilinear portico, and behind this portico at the top, on the central axis of the *cavea*, are two rooms whose function is not specifically known, though they are certainly in some sense ritualistic. The interior of one is furnished with a bench along three sides and may have served for the sacred banquets which are known to have been an element in some of the Syrian cults.[44] This sanctuary, incidentally, was certainly known to the Romans of the first century B.C., and it is likely that Pompey saw this "theater" on the same trip home from the Mithridatic campaigns during which he visited Mytilene.

There is only one example known of such a sanctuary in North Africa, at Dugga, but its presence shows that there was at least some Punic importation of this theatrical element of Syrian religion into Africa; it is further significant in its form, which differs from both the Dura and the Houran type of sanctuary.[45] In the Dugga complex the temple, consisting of an apsed *cella* with a vestibule in front, is above and on the central axis of the theater-like *cavea*. The two are separated by a porticoed court on a level midway between them, and there is direct communication between all three elements of the complex. The disposition is reminiscent of the Cagliari sanctuary discussed above (pp. 32-33) and architecturally suggests the Roman *cavea* shrine, while the sanctuaries found in central Syria do not.

It is impossible to specify the influence exerted on the Roman theaters by the non-Roman religious connection of theater and temple reflected in the architectural complexes described above.[46] One thing, however, may be stated with certainty; a

---

ditions possible, les cérémonies qui se déroulaient devant la porte même de la chapelle proprement dite, où se dressait l'image de la divinité. Et si l'on y regarde de près, le dispositif de Si', Sur, et Sahr est pratiquement le même: le théâtre est formé par la cour qui s'étend devant le temple véritable. La différence est dans l'échelle des monuments et dans leur forme architecturale." (*Annales arch. de Syrie*, I, 76)

[43] Detailed description and discussion *ibid.*, pp. 59-79, with plan, p. 60.

[44] *Ibid.*, pp. 74-75.

[45] Charles-Picard, *Les religions de l'Afrique antique*, pp. 160-161.

[46] M. Edmond Frézouls, in personal correspondence, has expressed some hesitation over this "rapprochement." He considers the "théâtres cultuels" a phenomenon limited to the interior of Syria and not properly Phoenician. In this case, however, the temple-theater complex at Dugga must be considered to belong to another tradition, and I should prefer to regard it, more simply, as reflecting Syrian-Phoenician religious influence. It would be well to emphasize that I am here considering the Syrian "théâtre cultuel" as a religious, rather than as an architectural tradition. M. Frézouls has rightly reminded me that the "tradition théatrale" in Africa is "purement romaine et sans rapports avec le passé carthaginois"; that is, the construction of the secular theater building in North Africa is linked exclusively to the introduction of Roman civilization. I should not, for example, wish to propose that the Roman theaters with *cavea* shrine were a typological development from the Syrian cult theaters. However, I should not consider it an unreasonable

familiarity with the idea of the combination of theater and shrine in a religious sphere would lead a provincial people to accept more naturally and build more readily the manifestation of that combination in a more secularized form: the Roman theater with a *cavea* shrine surmounting it.

Instances of the *cavea* shrine seem scarcer in the other provinces of the Empire. However, the best example extant, with Leptis Magna, is in Gallia Narbonensis, at Vienne (Fig. 32).[47] Built about 15 B.C., contemporaneous with the theaters at Arles, Orange, and Vaison,[48] the theater at Vienne is the largest in Gaul. The structure is well preserved, although unfortunately much of the superstructure of the *cavea* has been hidden in remodeling the theater for modern outdoor drama festivals. At the top of the *cavea*, with its portico on a line with the colonnade encircling the auditorium, is a shallow temple with *pronaos* and *cella* and four columns *in antis*.[49] The porch is completed by square engaged pilasters at the ends of the *antae*, making the temple seemingly hexastyle. The temple protruded about one and a half meters behind the circumference wall of the auditorium, ending in a straight wall. Its exact dimensions are given by the cutting of the rock behind and by the straight section breaking the curve of the wall of the third deambulatory in front, 13.95 meters wide and 8.80 meters deep. It is thus considerably larger than the *cavea* shrines of the African provinces, perhaps in proportion to the relatively larger size of the theater. The *cella* is extremely shallow in proportion to its width (2.50 by 11.70 meters) and includes a statue base on the axis against the rear wall. It was approached through a narrow door from the porch.

The system of approach to the temple is noteworthy.[50] The shrine was cut off by the side walls of the porch from the portico above the *cavea*, and because of a considerable difference in level was not directly approachable from the central aisle of the auditorium. Instead, there was an entrance from this central aisle into the vaulted deambulatory between the top of the second *maenianum* and the portico. From here two staircases taking off from the middle of the deambulatory give lateral access to the narrow terrace defined by the roof of the deambulatory vault. Above this another vault, existing only here at the central point of the terrace, indicates the presence of a level platform along the front of the temple, approachable from another set of stairs from the terrace, perhaps converging at the center of the plat-

supposition that the Roman theaters on some occasion may have been used *as if* they were. In his article on the Roman theaters of Syria, Frézouls has strongly, and in my opinion correctly, emphasized the difference between the Greek, the Roman, and the Syrian connections between theater and temple. "La Grèce n'a pas connu cette association systématique du théâtre et du temple, très différente, d'un autre coté, de celle qui a existé en Occident [the Roman sphere]." (*Annales arch. de Syrie*, ii, 86)

[47] The theater was excavated between 1922 and 1938 under the direction of Jules Formigé, who has published it in a short monograph, *Le théâtre romain de Vienne*.

[48] Formigé, "Remarques sur les dates de construction des théâtres d'Arles, d'Orange et de Vienne," *Mélanges Picard*, pp. 382-386.

[49] Described in detail in Formigé, *Le théâtre romain de Vienne*, pp. 9-11, with plan, fig. 30.

[50] *Ibid.*, p. 8.

form. Traffic could pass along the terrace under this platform. The floor of the shrine itself was raised 0.75 meters above the pavement of the platform in front, a factor which would increase the visibility of both the temple from below and the theater from the temple. The difference was probably made up by three steps leading up from the platform. The façade of the temple, as well as the interior, was completely revetted in white marble. No fragments attributable to the pediment have been found,[51] but two tiles of gilt bronze found nearby come probably from its covering. It may have been crowned by an acroterion.[52] Given a height proportionate to its ground dimensions it would have dominated by several feet the colonnade crowning the rest of the *cavea*. One notices again the emphasis on the axiality of the monument, strongly brought out at Vienne by the especially dominant *aula regia* of the stage building and continued through to a stepped and monumentalized street entrance from the narrow portico behind the stage.[53]

The strange fragments of capitals found on the site of this temple permit us to identify the divinity honored there with relative certainty (Fig. 33). They show serpents curled around a central tripod, with their coils forming the volutes of the composite style capitals. Underneath are acanthus leaves.[54] The iconography unmistakably suggests Apollo, who is singularly appropriate to an Augustan monument, in addition to whatever aptness he had in regard to theaters and *ludi scaenici*.[55]

At Lillebonne (Juliobona) in Gallia Belgica, the small Roman theater contains a feature not unlike the *cavea* shrines described above but in a different position (Fig. 34).[56] The first rows of the *cavea* are interrupted, at the midpoint of the semicircle, by a level room enclosed with three heavy walls and opening only on the front toward the orchestra. The rear wall of this room, which follows the curve of the auditorium, was decorated with two engaged columns, while the façade of the structure was formed by two free-standing columns and two engaged columns at the ends of the side walls. The pavement was on a level with the orchestra seats. The room was decorated with marble but there is no trace of the roofing or of the trabeation above the façade. Navarre suggests that when the theater was later changed into an *oppidum* for protection against invaders, this structure was built as a private *loggia* for the chief magistrate of the city.[57] However, although this ele-

---

[51] "Sans doute y voyait-on Apollon, peut-être entouré des Muses, comme sur un relief du musée d'Arles. Sa tête pouvait-être radiée, comme sur un relief trouvé dans le Rhône à Vienne." (*Ibid.*, p. 10)

[52] Formigé (*ibid.*, p. 11) suggests the identification of a temple depicted on a small relief in the Vienne museum with the theater shrine. The relief temple is crowned with an acroterion.

[53] See plan, fig. 32.

[54] *Ibid.*, p. 10 and figs. 24-26. Three other capitals of the same type are in the Vienne museum.

[55] See Gagé, *Apollon romain*, pp. 395-407.

[56] Caumont, *Abécédaire ou rudiment d'archéologie, ère gallo-romaine*, pp. 312-314; Wieseler, *Theatergebäude*, pp. 21-22 and pl. II, 18; Lantier, "La ville romaine de Lillebonne," *RA*, Ser. IV, Vol. XXI (1913), 201.

[57] "Le théâtre romain de Lillebonne," *REA*, XV (1913), 428.

ment is probably later than the original construction of the theater because of the presence of reused blocks with first century relief sculpture in the foundation, it is certainly still possible to interpret it as a shrine. The columned façade, in fact, seems to make this the most likely interpretation.

A theater-temple combination of strange shape that would need to be confirmed by further excavation is located at "Les Arènes de Tintignac" near Tulle.[58] Here nineteenth century drawings show an elaborate temple *temenos,* approximately semicircular, tangent to the *cavea* of the theater, with the main shrine at the rear of the semicircle on the central axis of the whole monument.

The heavily restored theater at Vaison-la-Romaine may possibly have provided another Gallic example of a theater shrine at the summit of the *cavea.*[59] At this point the theater has been reconstructed with external stairs supported on walls extending beyond the circumference of the *cavea,* and converging onto a narrow platform outside a central doorway leading into the portico which surrounds the top of the auditorium.[60] One is at least tempted to suggest the possible consideration of another reconstruction, based on a reconsideration of the material evidence with the now not unexampled existence of a *cavea* shrine in mind.

In Spain, the Roman theater at Saguntum has a level platform, approximately five meters wide and six meters deep, which interrupts the four rows of the *summum maenianum* on the central axis of the *cavea* (Fig. 35).[61] Apparently no traces of a superstructure covering this rectangular area have been found, but the possibility of its serving as an entrance is ruled out by the fact that the space is blocked at the back by the preserved circumference wall of the *cavea.* Entrances from the rear are in fact found on both sides of the platform with steps near them leading down over the *summum maenianum* to the *praecinctio* just in front of the platform. A base, interpreted as the pedestal of a statue but conceivably for an altar, stood at the front of this platform.[62] If for a statue, the figure would look directly down the central aisle of the auditorium to the orchestra below. This is almost certainly a modification of the *cavea* shrine.

[58] Johannès Plantadis, "Les arènes dites de Tintignac," *REA,* xv (1913), 434-436, with sketch plan, p. 434.

[59] The fullest description is in Sautel, *Vaison dans l'antiquité,* I, 235-254, with photographs and plans before restoration in Vol. III ("Recueil documentaire"), pls. LXXXIX-XCIII. For the theater after its restoration see Sautel, *Vaison-la-Romaine,* pp. 47-54, and especially the aerial photograph, p. 54.

[60] Actually the remains must have been extremely slight. "Au-delà [above the first *praecinctio*] nous ne pouvons plus rien affirmer, car les constructions ont été pillées et devastées par les bâtisseurs des siècles suivants, et cette partie du monument établie, comme nous l'avons dit, sur la mollasse de moins en moins consistante, n'a laissé aucune trace." (Sautel, *Vaison dans l'antiquité,* I, 240) Some trace of an unusual nature, however, near the middle of the rear must have led to the restoration of the strange entrance system, which is unparalleled in Gaul.

[61] Mélida, *Arqueologia Española,* p. 288; and Puig i Cadafalch, *L'Arquitectura romana a Catalunya,* pp. 196-201, with plan, fig. 254.

[62] Mélida, p. 288; Puig i Cadafalch, p. 198.

In the theater at Nicopolis in Epirus there is a strange, hitherto unexplained architectural element joined to the outside of the *cavea* on its central axis (Fig. 36).[63] Externally it seems to support a pair of lateral staircases, which do not, however, join at the top but leave between them a rectangular area several meters wide. If the vaulted structure below is finished with a level platform, this might be regarded as support for a shrine at the top of the auditorium. The lower part of the projection, however, on ground level, is carefully finished as a rectangular, cross-vaulted chamber, with a door on each side giving access outside the theater and a wide door at the front leading to the outer of the *ambulacri* under the *cavea*. Its most interesting feature is a semicircular niche or small apse at the back of the chamber on the axis. This seems to suggest the presence of more than a simple vestibule, and one is extremely tempted to see in this projection behind the theater at Nicopolis, probably of Augustan date, the archaeological remains of yet another example of a theater shrine.[64]

At Apamea, in Syria, the large Roman theater, although only partially excavated, furnishes a hint that here too may have existed another axial *cavea* shrine.[65] A trial trench has revealed one of the two radial supporting walls flanking the central axis of the *cavea* near the circumference wall. Enough of the wall was excavated to show that it is not convergent.[66] Therefore, assuming symmetry, a rectangular element at the top and rear of the *cavea* is indicated.

A coin from Heracleia in Bithynia probably provides an ancient graphic representation of a theatrical *cavea* shrine and adds another site to the list of examples of such shrines. Such is the most likely interpretation of the coin's iconography, although the building is sometimes regarded as a stadium and the small temple-like structure which rises above the colonnade at the top of the *cavea* is regarded by Wieseler as a tribunal.[67] Its façade is pictured as tetrastyle and is surmounted by a pediment.

In Italy itself one may observe several scattered examples of the *cavea* shrine.[68]

[63] Baccin and Ziino, "Nicopoli d'Epiro," *Palladio*, IV (1940), 5-6, and plan, fig. 11. The authors consider the structure only as a system of access, and the lower story as "una sorta di vestibolo."

[64] A second, larger, theater at Nicopolis may also be mentioned here, although it has not been excavated or thoroughly studied. Baccin and Ziino (*Palladio*, IV, 13) write, "sull'asse del teatro, all'esterno, si notano traccie di un avancorpo, con un ampia porta centrale, il quale poteva forse contenere una delle scale di accesso."

[65] Mayence, "La VIe campagne de fouilles à Apamée," *AntCl*, VIII (1939), 206-208. Frézouls, *Annales arch. de Syrie*, II, 52-53, gives a brief description of the theater, which is nearly as large as Pompey's, but makes no mention of the possibilities of a rectangular element at the rear of the *cavea*.

[66] This is observable from the plan of the excavated portions (Mayence, *AntCl*, VIII, pl. IX, fig. 13).

[67] See Donaldson, *Architectura Numismatica*, No. 75; and Wieseler, *Theatergebäude*, p. 31 and pl. III, 17.

[68] It is impossible within the present scope to make a complete and systematic study of the theaters in Italy. Moschella, in connection with a brief article on the theater at Gubbio, has published a partial list by regions (without bibliography) of the sites in Italy which include some

The best preserved of these, and perhaps the most interesting, is in the Villa Adriana near Tivoli. It has received almost no attention in recent times, however, because it lies in the "Academy," a portion of the Imperial villa outside the archaeological park and almost never visited.[69] To supplement the ruins which are now visible one may consult eighteenth and early nineteenth century descriptions and plans by Ligorio, Contini, Piranesi, Nibby, and Pannini (Figs. 37 and 38).[70] The structure has not been systematically excavated. The theater as a whole shows the regular Roman semicircular groundplan with a quite elaborately articulated (and well-preserved) stage building. At the center of the top of the *cavea*, just outside the line of the circumference wall, which is broken here, are the remains of a high-walled circular structure open at the front, about six meters in diameter. The floor level of the shrine is not that of the top of the *cavea*, but rather that of a *praecinctio* separating the last few rows of the auditorium from the lower ones. From earlier descriptions we may complete the plan with a trapezoidal level platform of considerable size in front of the shrine, and some system of access stairs behind it on both sides.[71] Rather than a single center aisle leading up to the platform there seem to have been two aisles so arranged as to continue up to the back of the *cavea* on either side of the area reserved for the platform. In the matter of the details and decorative elements connected with this shrine it is necessary to use the earlier descriptions with a certain caution. There is nothing intrinsically unlikely, however, in Sebastiani's notation of a pedestal for a statue centrally located in the *aedicula* near the rear wall,[72] especially since there are extant parallels in other theater shrines. Nor is there any specific reason to distrust Ligorio's statement that the temple was preceded by a paved vestibule with a façade of four columns, and that this was decorated with statues, of which one was a Hercules figure.[73] In general, the feature which sets this

vestiges of a theater or theaters (*Dioniso*, VII [1939], 15-16). The list includes 116 sites, most of which are quite insufficiently published. Few even of the published ones have been sufficiently excavated to reveal details of their structure. Obviously, completeness can not be obtained in this area. Research should be considerably aided when M. Frézouls completes the study on which he writes that he is now engaged, "sur l'histoire du type architectural du théâtre romain, tel qu'il s'est formé en Italie."

[69] It was mentioned, however, by Dorothy Kent Hill in her article on Pompey's theater-temple (*CJ*, XXXIX, 361). She cites Wieseler, *Theatergebäude*.

[70] Ligorio's plans, unpublished, were used as the basis for a corrected plan and description by Contini (*Pianta della Villa Tiburtina*, Rome, 1751). Piranesi's plan is reproduced in Canina, *Architettura antica*, III, pl. CX, from which comes Wieseler, *Theatergebäude*, pl. II, no. 13, and Winnefeld, *Die Villa des Hadrian bei Tivoli*, p. 123, fig. 40. Nibby's discussion is in *Dintorni di Roma*, III, 699-701. Pannini's very elaborate plans are published in Sebastiani, *Viaggio a Tivoli*, Foligno, 1828, which I have not been able to consult. The reproduction in fig. 38 is taken from a slide in the collection of the University of Michigan Department of Classical Studies.

[71] Pannini's and Piranesi's plans both show two pairs of steps from the rear, one leading up around the curve of the shrine onto the platform in front and the other following the lines of the two convergent aisles nearest the center of the *cavea*.

[72] Quoted in Wieseler, *Theatergebäude*, p. 18. It is unlikely that any evidential weight should be attached to his suggestion that the statue was "forse di Apollo."

[73] "Ligorio che vide questo teatro in uno stato di miglior conservazione ci assicura che

shrine off from others which have been observed, in addition to its circular form, is the unusually large platform in front of it. This might be regarded as an Imperial box or *Hauptloge* in front of the shrine, though there is no possibility of regarding the circular building itself as such,[74] since the narrow door and its position at the back of a long level platform would cut off the visibility to the stage of anyone seated within.[75]

Together with the theater in Hadrian's Villa must be mentioned two other examples, similar in structure, offered by private villas. In the smaller of two theaters in the villa at Pausilypon the two last rows of the lower *maenianum* are interrupted by a comparatively large level platform with a room enclosed on three sides at the back and an open area in front (Figs. 39 and 40).[76] In the rear wall is an apse in which a statue pedestal was found. In the middle of the room is a small elevation which has been taken to indicate "the Imperial seat or pulvinar."[77] The walls of the apse show iron studs which held a marble revetment. The room was approached through two passages from the sides, enclosed at either end by a door and decorated with colored plaster.[78] The presence of the apse and the parallel of Hadrian's Villa seem to indicate that this is not simply a secular loggia, although the area in front of the enclosed shrine may again have functioned as a box for important personages.

Still a third example of the same arrangement may be seen in the tiny theater belonging to the villa of M. Agrippa Postumus on the island of Planasia (Pianosa) in the Tuscan archipelago. Again the so-called Imperial box has a semicircular apse at its rear and is fronted by two columns.[79]

At Casinum in southern Latium another *cavea* temple has been discovered, of a more standard type than the shrines in the villa theaters.[80] It stood at the mid-

---

quattro colonne striate di ordine jonico di due palmi di diametro e 18 di altezza formavano il vestibolo, o prospetto di questo tempietto; che il suo pavimento era a scudetti romboidali, lunghi ciascuno 1 piede, e larghi mezzo, di marmi rosso, giallo, bianco e verde alternati; e che sopra suggesti erano tre statue, una delle quali fu di Ercole, come ricavossi dai frammenti trovati." (Nibby, *Dintorni di Roma*, III, 700) In Winnefeld, *Die Villa des Hadrian bei Tivoli*, p. 125, it is further specified that Ligorio's identification of one of the statues as Hercules was based on the remains of a club found on the base near the right foot.

[74] Cf. Wieseler, *Theatergebäude*, p. 18.

[75] Canina's plan of the Villa as a whole (*Architettura antica*, III, pl. CCXLII) also shows a quite large temple surmounting the *cavea* of the "Greek Theater" near the present park entrance. However, there seems to be no other evidence for its existence, and one must remain skeptical with Nibby (*Dintorni di Roma*, III, 666): "Piranesi immagina un tempio di Nettuno anfiprostilo peristilo sul centro della cavea; di questo non rimane alcun indizio."

[76] Wieseler, p. 15, and pl. II, 9b; Günther, *Pausilypon*, pp. 40-47; Touring Club Italiano, *Guida d'Italia—Napoli e dintorni*, p. 289.

[77] Günther, p. 42; Wieseler, p. 15, calls it "eine sitzähnliche Erhöhung."

[78] These comparatively elaborate closed passages are difficult to explain, unless they are simply an extravagance based on the private nature of the villa theater and the shrine area.

[79] See Pietro Moschella, "Teatri minori della settima regione," *Dioniso*, VIII (1940), 47-48, with plan.

[80] See Fuhrmann in *AA*, LVI (1941), cols. 554-560; Carettoni, *Casinum* (*Italia romana: municipi e colonie*), Ser. I, Vol. II, pp. 83-88 with photo tav. VI and plan tav. VIII; and Caret-

point of the portico which surmounted the vaulted *ambulatio* at the back of the auditorium, and was itself directly over a rectangular entrance into that vaulted passage. It is revealed on the ground plan only by a projection of the circumference wall to the rear at either side of the entrance, finished in a straight line. The whole is not wider than five meters. The original construction of the theater is datable to the Augustan period, but renovations attributable to the second half of the first century A.D. may have included the portico and perhaps the temple.[81]

One of the most striking instances of all the theater shrines is at Herculaneum, which provides the only now discoverable parallel to the multiplicity of shrines found in the theater of Pompey (Fig. 41).[82] Furthermore, Herculaneum provides the best possible example of the elaborate decorative elements which could be part of a Roman theater since so much of the statuary and architectural decoration, including many fragments of bronze statues, was found at or near its original location, only to be destroyed or removed after it was found.[83] The excavation was carried out during the eighteenth century, mostly by the technique of tunneling through and under the lava, and consequently the theater is almost completely inaccessible to investigation today. Ruggiero's study, based on available excavation diaries and records, gives the following extremely valuable information about those portions of the theater pertinent to this study:

The circle of these last rows of seats is partly interrupted by the three pairs of large pedestals decorated with marble and jutting forward, one in the middle of the semicircle and two at the extremes, on which rested six equestrian statues of gilded bronze, recovered in fragments and all six destroyed, with no notice other than the fact that two of the horsemen had their swords at their sides (March 17, 1739). These pedestals formed, in pairs, the sides of three *aediculae*—or, as we might say, tabernacles—noted by Weber from October 22 to 29, 1763; by la Vega on July 6, 1765; and more recently (as de Jorio tells on p. 120) by Mazois, who believed himself to have been the first to have seen them; but perhaps through poor observation he drew in his restoration four columns along the front, which the narrowness of the space would not have allowed. From one side of the middle shrine there still remains the base and drum of a stucco column painted red. From the right-hand shrine there remains *in situ* an Attic base of marble, and below, on the steps of the *cavea*, were recovered a statue of a Vestal Virgin, two fragments of inscriptions, two column drums of Africano, and two Corinthian capitals of marble. Behind the left-hand shrine, where the flow of the torrent had carried it, a column of portasanta had been thrown outside the theater. Nothing can be conjectured of their form and structure, because of lack of light from the documents, except that in the right-hand shrine probably stood the Vestal, and more certainly, according to the Accademici Ercolanesi, the Nero Claudius Drusus stood

toni, *NSc*, Ser. VI, Vol. XV, 99-141. Only Fuhrmann mentions the temple, calling it "eine kleine tempelartige 'Ädikula'" (col. 555).

[81] Carettoni, *Casinum*, pp. 87-88; and Fuhrmann in *AA*, LVI, cols. 559-560.

[82] See above, p. 53.

[83] "The number of fragments of decorative marble, and of bronze and marble statues, recorded in the excavators' journals, is almost incredible. . . . They left it a stripped and mutilated skeleton." (Waldstein, *Herculaneum*, p. 70)

in one of the others; and perhaps each of the three, in the pediment or elsewhere, had as decoration one of the large scenic masks of peperino finished with stucco, found on April 10, 1739, March 17, 1770, and April 25, 1772.[84]

The construction dates from the early years of the Empire,[85] and it is difficult not to see here the influence of Rome and the theater of Pompey, although, to be sure, the Herculaneum theater contained three shrines of equal size (though not of equal weight, since the central one would be psychologically dominant), while the Roman theater contained one dominant temple to Venus and four subsidiary shrines. It would be hopeless to try to identify the divinities honored here at Herculaneum. The only possible hints come from identifiable statue fragments, which include, in addition to numerous marble and bronze portraits of the Imperial family and local benefactors, fragments of a bronze Hercules and a small marble Venus.[86]

In 1950 excavations at Sepino, in Samnite territory, brought to light remains at the back of the theater which almost certainly indicate the presence of another example of the *cavea* shrine (Fig. 42).[87] The city wall runs obliquely past the back of the theater, and the circumference wall of the auditorium touches it near its midpoint. Outside the city wall at this point the remains of the beginning of a rectangular structure are visible, with a row of pilasters on its outside face. The structure must belong to the theater and not the wall, since it is aligned with the central axis of the *cavea* and senselessly oblique with respect to the city wall. If carried inside this wall and tied to the *cavea*, as it must be,[88] this structure would serve perfectly

[84] "Interrompevano in parte il giro di questi ultimi gradi le tre coppie di grandi piedestalli ornati di marmi e sporgenti in fuori, una nel mezzo del semicerchio e due dagli estremi, su cui posavano sei statue equestri di bronzo dorato, ricolte in frantumi e distrutte tutte e sei, senz'altra notizia che due dei cavalieri avevano la spada al fianco (17 marzo 1739). Questi cosiffatti piedestalli a due a due mettevano in mezzo tre *aediculae* o come noi diciamo tabernacoli, avvertiti dal Weber a 22 e 29 ottobre 1763, da la Vega a 6 luglio 1765 e più recentemente dal Mazois, come narra il de Jorio a pag. 120, che credette essere stato il primo a ravvisarli; ma forse non bene osservandoli disegnò nel restauro quattro colonne nel fronte, che per la strettezza del luogo non vi potrebbero capire. Del tabernacolo di mezzo resta ancora da un lato la base e il mozzicone di una colonna di stucco colorata in rosso; dell'altro a destra avanza parimente sul posto una base attica di marmo e, appiedi, sopra i gradi della *cavea* fu raccolta la statua della Vestale, due frammenti d'iscrizioni, due fusti di colonne di africano e due capitelli corintii di marmo. Alle spalle del tabernacolo sinistro, come portava la corsìa del torrente era stata gettata fuori del Teatro una colonna di portasanta. Nè della loro forma e struttura si può nulla congetturare, perchè altro lume non dànno i documenti, se non che sotto il tabernacolo a man destra era probabilmente la Vestale, e più certamente, secondo gli Accademici Ercolanesi, sotto a uno degli altri due il Nerone Claudio Druso; e forse ciascuno dei tre, nel fastigio o altrove, aveva per finimento una delle grandi maschere sceniche di piperno rivestite di stucco, trovate a 10 aprile 1739, 17 marzo 1770 e 25 aprile 1772." *Storia degli scavi di Ercolano*, p. xxv; cf. the shorter notices, p. xviii and p. xxi.

[85] Waldstein, *Herculaneum*, p. 70.

[86] Ruggiero, *Storia degli scavi di Ercolano*, p. 3 and p. 38.

[87] Description of the theater in Cianfarani, "Sepino—Teatro, campagna di scavo 1950," *NSc*, Ser. VIII, Vol. V (1951), 88-106, with plan, p. 88.

[88] The area inside the city wall at the rear of the *cavea* was not yet excavated at the time of the publication.

for the foundation of a *cavea* temple projecting behind the theater, like that of the theater of Pompey.[89]

At Fiesole the Roman theater is dominated by a very large platform above the back of the *cavea* which consists of a central area approximately twenty meters wide and ten meters deep flanked by two narrow passages on each side, one leading directly into the top rows of the *cavea* and the other leading down by means of stairs to a path outside the circumference wall of the auditorium (Fig. 43).[90] The function of the central area is not known.[91] It probably contained a colonnade and perhaps substituted for a portico around the top of the *cavea*. The possibility of a partly religious function should not be disregarded, however, in view of its similarity in position to other examples considered above, and in view of an altar found on the central axis of the theater *cavea*.[92]

The theater at Faleria has a solid rectangular substructure contiguous to the outside wall of the *cavea* at its midpoint (Fig. 44).[93] According to the plan given in Wieseler[94] the foundation is not large enough to support a regular shrine, and is best regarded as a statue base, especially since many fragments of bronze statuary were found nearby. It is not known whether or not there was a level platform in front of this base.

Thus some twenty examples, certain or probable, of the *cavea* shrine have been adduced for the Roman world subsequent to the construction of the theater of Pompey.[95] Geographically, they have been found in most parts of the Roman sphere, although the eastern half of the Empire accounts for only two likely cases, and North Africa accounts for a proportionately high number. Chronologically, their dates of

[89] Cianfarani, who mentions the possibility that this is the foundation for a "sacello," gives no information regarding the absolute or relative dating of the theater and the wall. It would seem, because of the peculiar and somewhat inefficient construction of the foundations partly on the outside and partly on the inside of the wall, that the shrine came as an afterthought after the main semicircle of the *cavea* had been constructed, or at least after it had been begun.

[90] Wieseler, *Theatergebäude*, pp. 20-21, 27, pls. II, 17 and III, 11 c; Lombardi, *Faesulae* (*Italia romana: municipi e colonie*, Ser. I, Vol. IV), pp. 56-63; Minto, "I teatri romani di Firenze e di Fiesole," *Dioniso*, VI (1937), 4-7.

[91] "Gewiss hatte die mittlere und wichtigste Abtheilung derselben die Bestimmung einer Loge," Wieseler, p. 27. Minto (*Dioniso*, VI, 6) and Lombardi (*Faesulae*, p. 57) regard it as a porticoed terrace serving as an entrance vestibule.

[92] Minto, *Dioniso*, VI, 5.   [93] Wieseler, pp. 19-20.   [94] *Ibid.*, pl. II, 15.

[95] Three possible instances in Italy have not been mentioned in the text because the nature of the evidence is too vague and uncertain. One is at Libarna, where the publication (Moretti, "Serravalle Scrivia—Scavi nell'area della città di Libarna," *NSc*, 1914, pp. 127-134) indicates a large central *parodos* with two lateral apses; but no part of the upper structure remains. Another is the theater at Padua, explored during the eighteenth century, where the plan shows certain projections from the *cavea* at the ends and midpoint, but where subsequent excavation seems to indicate that these actually belong to a second *maenianum* (Gasparotto, *Padova romana*, pp. 119-121). A third is in Latium at Bovillae, where earlier not entirely trustworthy plans by Canina and Angelini show walls at the back of the theater *cavea* possibly capable of interpretation as a *cavea* shrine, but where the presently visible ruins are insufficient to support any interpretation of this area (Al. Dobosi, "Bovillae," *EphDac*, VI [1935], 257-299 with fig. 11, p. 293 and fig. 48, p. 352).

construction range from the Augustan period to the early third century. They show considerable variety in form. In some, the rear wall is flush with the rear wall of the theater *cavea* (Leptis Magna, Tipasa, Saguntum, and probably Apamea and Herculaneum); in others the temple is built almost entirely beyond the circumference wall of the *cavea*, like Pompey's temple of Venus Victrix (Dugga, Timgad, Nicopolis, Sepino, Hadrian's Villa); in many the shrine projects only partly beyond the rest of the *cavea* (Calama, Philippeville, Cherchel, Vienne, Vaison, Casinum). In a few cases it may be located lower in the *cavea* (Lillebonne, Pausilypon). The rear wall in some cases contains an apse, as in Pompey's theater temple (Calama, Nicopolis, Pausilypon, Pianosa).[96] In one case the shrine is circular (Hadrian's Villa). There is no apparent correlation between these differences in form and the place or time of construction of the theaters. What is common to all is a location on the central axis of the theater overlooking the orchestra with the front facing the stage building, with provision for a statue of the divinity.[97] Most have a colonnaded façade and many are approachable by special steps or entrances through the back wall of the *cavea*.[98]

[96] A. W. Van Buren ("L'abside nel tempio Romano," *Atti4CStR*, II [1938], 134-137) suggests that the apsed temple in Roman architecture was originally and especially intended "non per il culto delle grandi divinità nazionali, ma per culti più intimi, familiari, o perfino individuali." He lists examples in Pompeii which support his contention and then adduces the parallels of the temples of the Roman Imperial fora—Venus Genetrix, Mars Ultor, and Minerva—which may with justification be said to represent "culti familiari" nationalized through their relation to the emperor. Pompey's temple of Venus Victrix, which Van Buren mentions, falls into the type, and this might provide a hint for identifying the kind of cult, though not the specific divinity, honored by the theater shrines with this feature. Such a connection would be appropriate in any case for the villa theaters.

[97] Though there are not always archaeological remains of statue bases (as there are at, e.g., Leptis Magna and Vienne) it seems reasonable to assume that this was an invariable feature.

[98] For a discussion of other architectural combinations of theater and temple, in addition to the *cavea* shrine, see the Appendix.

CHAPTER V
POMPA, SELLISTERNIUM, AND ALTAR

"ad scaenam a templis et aris" (Tert. *De Spect.* 10. 2)

POMPA, SELLISTERNIUM, AND ALTAR

IN ADDITION to the direct architectural or topographical connection between theater and temple discussed in the preceding chapter, there existed further bonds between the two, less direct but still physical, expressing themselves through the "trappings" of the *ludi scaenici*. A general lack of awareness among scholars of the existence of these bonds makes it imperative briefly to collect and discuss here the evidence that has come to light to the present time.

Roman theatrical presentations were regularly preceded by a sacred procession, a *pompa*. The nature of a Roman procession is well known through a long description in Dionysius of Halicarnassus and through the investigations of modern scholarship.[1] Its religious quality is well expressed in the following general description of the Greek procession, which will apply also to the Roman phenomenon:

> . . . a festival procession organized by the *polis* or a cult association; a god either accompanies the procession or stands at its end. Something is escorted, either the divinity or the offering. . . . The *pompa* is not an independent cult act but is only the prelude to such an act: the sacrifice, the bath of the god, or the sacred marriage.[2]

In addition we know many details of the Roman *pompa circensis*.[3] The parade included the prominent youth of the city, the contestants at the games, various troupes of dancers and musicians, persons carrying incense and perfumes and precious objects from the temple treasuries, and finally the gods, represented by statues or other symbols carried on special wagons called *tensae*. The procession ended with a sacrifice preceding the games themselves.

But one searches almost in vain among modern writers for any mention of the *pompa* in connection with the theater.[4] Only Lily Ross Taylor has insisted upon the recognition of its occurrence for *ludi scaenici* as well as *ludi circenses*.[5] The evidence,

---

[1] Dionysius (*Ant. Rom.* vii. 72) cites Fabius Pictor as his source, but interpolates details from his own experience. The description is studied in detail by Piganiol (*Recherches sur les jeux romains*, pp. 15-31), who attempts to disentangle its various elements. His conclusion is that the original presentation in Fabius was not a description of an actual *pompa*, but rather a copy of a document reflecting a suggested program for a *pompa*, "une sorte de procès-verbal du type de ces *Acta* qui nous ont été conservés, par exemple, pour les jeux séculaires." See the extensive article by Franz Bömer in *RE*, xxi, cols. 1878-1994, *s.v.* "Pompa," where the bibliography is cited.

[2] ". . . der festliche von der Polis oder einer Kultgemeinschaft ausgerichtete Zug mit oder zur Gottheit. Man geleitet, πέμπει . . . etwas, die Gottheit oder das Opfer. . . . Die Pompa ist auch keine selbständige kultische Handlung; sie ist nur der Zug zu einer solchen, diese steht am Ende der Pompa: das Opfer, das Bad der Gottheit, der ἱερὸς γάμος." (*Ibid.*, col. 1886)

[3] Piganiol, pp. 18-27.

[4] The article of Bömer (see above, n. 1) makes no mention of the fact, nor does that of Habel (*RE*, Suppl. v, cols. 608-630, *s.v.* "ludi publici"). Wissowa's *Religion und Kultus der Römer* is silent on the connection, nor do the general works on the Roman theater (e.g., Bieber, *History*; Oehmichen, *Das Bühnenwesen der Griechen und Römer*) even hint of its existence.

[5] "The 'Sellisternium' and the Theatrical 'Pompa,'" *CP*, xxx (1935), p. 128. In her unpublished paper referred to above (Chapter I, n. 34) she uses the phrase, "the *pompa* which opened both circus and theatrical games."

nonetheless, is incontrovertible. Tertullian, having previously described the *pompa* of the circus with all its religious symbols, remarks:

Now let us go on to matters of the theater. . . . Its apparatus is equal in this respect: there is a procession to the stage from the temples and the altars, with the same disgrace of incense and blood amid pipes and horns, under the leadership of those two most foul arbiters of funerals and sacrifices, the "dissignator" and the soothsayer.[6]

Sacred procession, sacrifice, and soothsayer, he assures the reader, are as much a part of stage presentations as they are of circus games. Equally unequivocal is the statement of Dionysius of Halicarnassus with regard to the dancers known as *ludiones*, who, he says, take part in "the processions, both those which take place in the circus and those which take place in the theaters."[7] Further independent evidence comes from the proof for the existence of one act of that theatrical *pompa*, the carrying of special chairs into the theater on performance days.

The *sellisternium*, a little known Roman rite which consisted in the preparation of chairs with cushions, drapery, and symbols of the gods, was formerly thought to have been a Roman supplement to the *lectisternium* for the benefit of the goddesses, who could not, according to the Roman custom, recline at banquets given in their honor but must sit instead.[8] The existence of coin representations of draped chairs with the symbols of male divinities—Jupiter and Neptune for example—is proof that this is not a sufficient explanation for the custom.[9] Evidence for another use of the draped chair comes mainly through references to a type of divine honor paid the Roman emperors.[10] The senate voted that Caesar's golden chair and crown be carried into the theater ἐξ ἴσου τοῖς τῶν θεῶν.[11] Instances of this honor are recorded for many living emperors and dead members of the Imperial family, of which the most interesting is the case of Commodus, when a lion's skin and club were placed as symbols on the chair to represent his self-identification with Hercules.[12] Generally the symbol was either a garland or a crown.[13] Where these seats were placed in the

---

[6] "Transeamus ad scaenicas res. . . . Apparatus etiam ex ea parte consortes, qua ad scaenam a templis et aris et illa infelicitate turis et sanguinis inter tibias et tubas itur duobus inquinatissimis arbitris funerum et sacrorum, dissignatore et haruspice." (*De Spect.* 10. 1-2) "Dissignator" is used both of a master of ceremonies at funerals and of the chief usher at the theaters.

[7] τὰς πομπὰς τάς τε ἐν ἱπποδρόμῳ καὶ τὰς ἐν τοῖς θεάτροις γινομένας. (*Ant. Rom.* ii. 71)

[8] Taylor, *CP*, xxx, 124-125.

[9] *Ibid.*, p. 122; and Aline L. Abaecherli, "Imperial Symbols on Certain Flavian Coins," *CP*, xxx (1935), pl. I (opp. p. 139), no. 1.

[10] The evidence is briefly mentioned by Lily Ross Taylor in "A Sellisternium on the Parthenon Frieze?" *Quantulacumque* ("Studies Presented to Kirsopp Lake"), pp. 253-254; and fully listed by her in *CP*, xxx, p. 127 and nn. 23-24.

[11] Cass. Dio xliv. 6. 3. From parallels it is clear that the crown was to be placed *on* the chair as a symbol. Compare the incident occurring at the circus games in A.D. 13 (Cass. Dio lvi. 29. 1) when a madman sat in Caesar's throne and put the crown which he took from the chair on his own head.

[12] Cass. Dio liii. 30. 6 (Marcellus); lviii. 4. 4 (Tiberius and Sejanus); lxxii. 31. 2 (Faustina); lxxiii. 17. 4 (Commodus); lxxv. 4. 1 (Pertinax); Tacitus *Ann.* ii. 83 (Germanicus).

[13] Abaecherli, *CP*, xxx, 135-138.

theater is difficult to ascertain although Miss Taylor believes they were in the orchestra together with the seats of the prominent senators and their wives.[14] She bases this on Lucretius iv. 78-80:

> namque ibi consessum caveai subter et omnem
> scaenai speciem patrum matrumque deorum
> inficiunt coguntque suo fluitare colore.[14a]

Adopting the manuscript reading, she explains the passage as describing the three main parts of a theater: *cavea*, stage, and orchestra, with the last containing the senators, matriarchs, and—in asyndeton—the gods, represented by their symbol-decked chairs. An interesting variant is proposed by Colin, who suggests that "patrum Matrisque deorum" be read in line 79, making the passage refer specifically to the Megalensian games.[15] Thus, in his view, a statue of Cybele would have watched the play,[16] although the words could still refer to the custom of the draped chair carried into the theater, a chair similar to that figured on the pediment of the Palatine temple of the Great Mother.[17] Bailey prints the end of line 79 between daggers, since none of the emendations proposed are paleographically feasible—except Merrill's "patrum matrumque decorem"[18]—and he is unwilling to accept Miss Taylor's interpretation of the text as it stands, apparently because he is unaware of the supporting evidence for the presence of gods in the theater.[19] With a knowledge of this evidence one must accept the text as it stands or Colin's emendation, depending on the view one holds on the presence of Roman matrons with their husbands in the first rank seats.[20] In either case, however, Lucretius provides a pre-Imperial reflection of the custom of placing symbols of the gods in the theater. One is inclined to accept the

[14] Lily Ross Taylor, "Lucretius on the Roman Theatre," *Studies in Honour of Gilbert Norwood*, p. 149.

[14a] "For there they [the awnings] tinge the assembly in the *cavea* below and all the outward form of the stage and of the fathers and the mothers and gods, and they force them to shimmer with their own color."

[15] Jean Colin, "Les sénateurs et la Mère des Dieux aux Megalesia: Lucrèce IV, 79," *Athenaeum*, XXXII (1954), 346-355.

[16] *Ibid.*, p. 352. "Il nous paraît très probable qu'une statue de Cybèle assistait à la représentation scénique du théâtre."

[17] See above, p. 15. In the unpublished paper there referred to (n. 34) Miss Taylor states that she and Dr. Aline Abaecherli Boyce missed this chair in their earlier discussion of the *sellisternium*, i.e., the articles in *CP*, XXX, 122-130 and 131-140. "The chair is important," she continues, "both as a significant example of a seat prepared for a divinity and also for its relation to Roman scenic games."

[18] *CPCP*, III (1916), 49.

[19] *De Rerum Natura*, ed. Cyril Bailey (Oxford, 1947), III, pp. 1189-90. In rejecting Miss Taylor's proposal he says, wrongly, that she does not "offer any evidence for the presence of such seated figures in the Roman theatre." Among the quainter proposed emendations are Bernay's "claram variamque deorsum" and Brieger's "Parium marmorque decorum."

[20] Bailey states, "they would not be sitting with the *patres*," and Miss Taylor can only offer one passage, Suetonius *Aug.* 44, of doubtful interpretation, in support of her contention that they did sit in the orchestra with their husbands "until Augustus revised the rules for seating." (*Studies in Honor of Gilbert Norwood*, p. 149 and n. 13)

general view of the passage as describing three separate portions of the building and to locate such symbols in the orchestra.

That these ritually prepared chairs were not permanent fixtures in the theater, or simply decorated at the site for the occasion, but were carried ceremonially in the *pompa* which preceded the *ludi* is clear from other evidence. Tertullian (*Ad nat.* i. 10) mentions *solisternia*—certainly a synonym for *sellisternia*—in connection with "sacri apparatus et tensae et currus," a collocation which probably suggests that the *solisternia* were used together with *tensae* and chariots, i.e., in a sacred procession.[21] But even more telling is the same author's description, ostensibly restricted to the procession before the circus games: "The *pompa* going before shows in itself to whom it belongs, with its row of *simulacra*, its column of *imagines*, its chariots, its *tensae*, its wagons, its chairs, its crowns, its *exuviae*."[22] In piling up the religious symbols used in the parades "which show in themselves whose procession this really is"—the devil's—Tertullian has actually confused the apparatus from two, or perhaps three, different types of *pompae*. It is likely that the chairs in the circus were permanent.[23] We know, at any rate, that the usual procedure in the *pompa circensis* was to carry the symbols of the gods, technically known as *exuviae*, in special carriages called *tensae*, while statues of the gods were also carried in chariots, or on *fercula*, trays borne on the shoulder.[24] They were not, apparently, carried on chairs.[25] Thus the *sedes* and the immediately following *coronae*—this was one of the most common forms of the divine or Imperial symbol placed on chairs—of Tertullian's description very probably are taken from the *pompa theatralis* and not the *pompa circensis*.

A recently discovered bronze tablet from Magliano is important evidence for the manner in which the ritual chair was used in connection with the theater.[26] The inscription records part of the decree honoring Germanicus after his death, providing a confirmation and elaboration of Tacitus *Ann.* ii. 83.[27] It is datable to the winter of A.D. 19/20. The text of the pertinent provision of the decree (lines 50-54) is as follows:

It is decreed that at the *ludi Augustales*, when the chairs of the *sodales* are placed in the theater, the curule chair of Germanicus Caesar is to be placed among them, with the oak crown, in his honor; the aforesaid chairs are to be brought forth from the temple of the

[21] The passage is so interpreted by Taylor (*CP*, xxx, 127-128).

[22] "Pompa praecedens, quorum sit in semetipsa probans de simulacrorum serie, de imaginum agmine, de curribus, de tensis, de armamaxis, de sedibus, de coronis, de exuviis." (*De Spect.* 7).

[23] Taylor, *CP*, xxx, 129.

[24] Johannes Regner, *RE*, Suppl. vii, cols. 1627-29, *s.v.* "Ludi circenses"; Piganiol, *Recherches sur les jeux romains*, pp. 25-26.

[25] Abaecherli, *CP*, xxx, 131.

[26] Published by Antonio Minto, *NSc*, Ser. viii, Vol. i (1947), 51-54 and tav. i. The following historical comment by Ugo Coli (*ibid.*, pp. 55-68) stops just short of the passage with which we are dealing.

[27] "sedes curules sacerdotum Augustalium locis superque eas querceae coronae statuerentur; ludos circensis eburna effigies praeiret. . . ." Without the comment of the inscription the passage could not be guaranteed to refer to the theater.

Deified Augustus when that temple shall have been completed; meanwhile they are to be put back into the temple of Mars Ultor and carried out from there; and whoever shall produce the aforesaid games shall see to it that the chairs be taken from the aforesaid temple to the theater, and, when they are to be removed, that they be replaced in that temple.[28]

Thus the decree provides confirmation for the fact that the chairs were actually carried into the theater. In this instance it is further stated that the chair was regularly to be kept in a temple, and the temple is the one which would be the only logical starting point for a procession connected with the *ludi Augustales*. Although in this case the chair belongs to a divinely honored mortal and not a god properly speaking, it seems reasonable to suggest that this was the regular procedure for the use of all such ritual chairs. Adding to this Tertullian's phrase "ad scaenam a templis" (*De Spect.* 10. 2), one may propose the following pattern of operations for the ceremony preceding *ludi scaenici*: at an appropriate temple, chairs of gods and specially honored mortals were prepared in a rite sometimes called a *sellisternium*; these were then carried from the temple to the theater or theaters as part of a procession which was carefully organized from a ritual standpoint;[29] upon reaching the theater they were placed in a position—in the orchestra, or, as in the case of Germanicus, in honorary seats in the *cavea* together with living members of his college—from which the god or honored mortal could watch the performance, through the medium of the symbol which represented him.

The use by Tertullian, in his description of the *pompa*, of the phrase "imaginum agmen" strongly suggests yet a third type of procession, the *pompa funebris*.[30] Of course it would be possible to take the words as approximately synonymous with the immediately preceding "simulacrorum series," but it seems rather more likely that Tertullian is using the word *imagines* in its more technical sense of "ancestral image" and the phrase "imaginum agmen" to describe the line of such images that were regularly carried in a funeral procession.[31] The connection of *ludi funebres* with theatrical presentations during the Republic has already been mentioned

[28] "Utiq(ue) Ludis Augustalibus cum subsellia sodalium/ponentur in theatris, sellae curules Germanici Caesaris inter ea ponantur cum querceis coronis in honorem/eius sacerdoti; quae sellae cum templum Divi Aug(usti) perfectum erit ex eo templo proferentur; interea in templo Martis Ultoris reponantur et inde proferantur; qui(que) cum(que) eos ludos q(ui) s(upra) s(cripti) s(unt) faciat uti ex eo templo q(ui) s(upra) s(criptum) e(st) in the/atris ponantur, et cum reponendae erunt in eo templo reponantur, curet."

[29] "Das Zeremoniell dieser Prozession war bis ins Einzelnste mit der pedantischen Genauigkeit des römischen Kultus vorgeschrieben, und ein kleiner Verstoss konnte die ganze Feier ungültig machen." (Friedländer, *Darstellungen aus der Sittengeschichte Roms*, II, pp. 44-45)

[30] For the regular occurrence of such *pompae* and a description of them, see Mau in *RE*, III, cols. 350-354, s.v. "Bestattung," and additional comments by Bömer (*RE*, XXI, cols. 1980-82) who classifies the Roman *pompae* into three principal categories: *triumphalis, funebris*, and *circensis*.

[31] The contrast between men and gods somewhat parallels the use by Pliny, *Epist.* x. 96. 6: "imaginem tuam [Traiani] deorumque simulacra." Compare Tac. *Ann.* ii. 73, "sine imaginibus et pompa," and iv. 9, "imaginum pompa."

above.[32] It is now possible to see how these *ludi scaenici* are also related to the conception of the presentation of plays in the sight of and for the pleasure of the honored "deity." At the end of the regular funeral *pompa* the corpse was placed on the *rostra* or a specially constructed platform in the Forum. The *imagines*, men bearing the wax masks of the ancestors of the deceased, also would take their places on the platform, probably sitting in curule thrones, to witness the *laudatio* and the various *ludi*, including the plays that may have been presented in the same spot.[33] They represented, of course, the actual presence of the dead ancestors,[34] much as the symbols on the ritual chairs described above represented gods and members of the Imperial family.

The concepts and practices here illustrated have Greek precedents. In the Great Dionysia at Athens the statue of Dionysos was carried in the processions which took place before the dramatic contests, and was brought into the theater to be a witness of those contests.[35] There is no evidence, however, that the statue was carried on a chair. But Philip of Macedon, at the celebration of his daughter's marriage was carried, through the medium of a statue, into the theater on a throne together with the images of the twelve Olympians.[36]

"Quanta praeterea sacra, quanta sacrificia praecedant, intercedant, succedant," asserts Tertullian (*De Spect.* 7. 3) of the *ludi circenses*. Sacrifices were an essential part of all Roman *ludi*, and there is direct evidence for their occurrence in connection with *ludi scaenici*. In the preserved record of the Secular games of 17 B.C. there are two direct collocations of sacrifice and theatrical performance: "Ludique noctu sacrificio confecto sunt commissi in scaena" (line 100); and "Ludis scaenicis dimissis . . . iuxta eum locum ubi sacrificium erat factum superioribus noctibus" (line 153).[37] Suetonius tells us that before beginning the games at the rededication of the theater of Pompey, Claudius "supplicavit apud superiores aedes,"[38] which probably implies a sacrifice. Josephus' account of the death of Caligula definitely shows that before the plays there was a sacrifice and further that this sacrifice was in the same location: "After the processions had taken place Gaius sacrificed to Augustus Caesar, in whose honor, indeed, these shows were celebrated; . . . after the sacrifice he turned to the show and sat down."[39]

---

[32] See p. 17.

[33] See Mau in *RE*, III, cols. 353-354.

[34] "Die den Toten geleitenden Träger der Ahnenmasken sind im Augenblick der Pompa die göttlichen Ahnen selbst." (Bömer in *RE*, XXI, col. 1981)

[35] See Arthur Pickard-Cambridge, *The Dramatic Festivals of Athens*, p. 58 and the references cited in n. 6. Also Taylor in *Quantulacumque*, p. 262, n. 40.

[36] Diod. xvi. 92. 5. Philip becomes σύνθρονος τοῖς δώδεκα θεοῖς.

[37] *CIL*, VI, 32323.

[38] *Claud.* 21. 1.

[39] Γάιος δὲ προόδων αὐτῷ γενομένων ἔθυσε τῷ Σεβαστῷ Καίσαρι, ᾧ δὴ καὶ τὰ τῆς θεωρίας ἤγετο. . . . μετὰ δὲ τὴν θυσίαν ἐπὶ τὴν θεωρίαν τραπεὶς ἐκαθέζετο. (*AJ* xix. 1. 13)

The occurrence of sacrifices demands the presence of an altar. From Tertullian's characterization of the theatrical *pompa* as "ad scaenam a templis et aris" (*De Spect.* 10. 2), one may certainly say that the altar might rather be found at the beginning of the procession, at some point not in or adjacent to the theater. The instances cited in the above paragraph, however, show that the altar sometimes stood at the same site as the theater. The examination of references to altars in the comedies of Plautus and Terence has not, understandably, shed any real light on the problem of the existence or use of altars beyond their employment as stage properties.[40] The view that an altar to Apollo Agyiaios was standard on the Roman stage seems to depend rather too heavily on the Hellenistic models of Roman comedy,[41] much as former views of Plautus' playwriting techniques drew largely from these nonexistent originals. As Saunders admits at the end of her treatment of the subject, "the whole question deserves . . . a thorough investigation,"[42] since the evidence from the plays simply cannot be reduced to a consistent pattern. Naturally, archaeological evidence cannot be brought to bear on the period of the temporary theater. But it can demolish the troublesome view, almost universally accepted, that there was no *thymele*,[43] or orchestral altar, in the Roman theater building.

Such a view has led Bailey to discredit one piece of literary evidence for the existence of an altar for sacrifices in the Roman theater in Lucretius: "And the stage has been freshly sprinkled with Cilician saffron, and the nearby altar exhales its Panchaean scents."[44] He was induced into the inconsistency of citing passages to verify the Roman custom of sprinkling the stage with saffron but characterizing the next line as "probably taken bodily from Epicurus."[45] Miss Taylor says that she doubts this, and her doubts are confirmed by archaeological remains.[46] The altar mentioned by Lucretius is not on the stage, but "propter," a characterization which certainly would suit the orchestra.

[40] The most complete discussion of the question is by Catharine Saunders, "Altars on the Roman Comic Stage," *TAPA*, XLII (1911), 91-103. The article is mainly devoted to disproving the traditional view that the Roman comic stage regularly had two altars, one to Liber and the other to the divinity for whom the particular *ludi* were given. Her view is accepted by Duckworth, *The Nature of Roman Comedy*, pp. 83-84.

[41] ". . . the evidence that the altar of Apollo was regularly found before the Greek house and that the normal setting of *fabulae palliatae* exhibited entrances to such houses, that Apollo was recognized as a patron of comedy. . . ." (Saunders, *TAPA*, XLII, 103, referring to the arguments developed pp. 92-95)

[42] *Ibid.*, p. 103.

[43] I am using the word here in the sense of an altar in the center of the orchestra, a sense which is not now accepted as valid by some scholars. (See Fensterbusch in *RE*, A6, 1, cols. 700-704, s.v. θυμέλη.) It is, however, a useful term here since it emphasizes a distinction between these orchestral altars and any concept of a nonfunctional altar as stage property.

[44] "Et cum scaena croco Cilici perfusa recens est
    araque Panchaeos exhalat propter odores." (ii, 416-417)

[45] *De Rerum Natura* (ed. Bailey), ii, p. 872.

[46] *Studies in Honour of Gilbert Norwood*, p. 151. In n. 30 (p. 155), however, she is unaware of the archaeological evidence cited below.

The recent excavations of the theater in Leptis Magna, in addition to exposing a well-documented *cavea* shrine and a temple behind the stage building, have also brought to light the remains of a permanent theatrical altar erected during the reign of Domitian.[47] It stood in the *conistra*—the first rows of seats which actually belong to the orchestra—on the central axis of the theater. It consists of an octagonal shaft standing on a square base and surmounted by a cornice, and was approximately 1.4 meters high. Unfortunately the top portion of the shaft is destroyed, together with that portion of the inscription which recorded the divinity to whom the altar was sacred. We know only that he was qualified with the adjective "Augusto."[48]

One other theater altar has been noted in North Africa, at Dugga. In this case it appears to have been located in the central niche of the *pulpitum*, on the level of orchestra and facing out toward the *cavea*. Nothing further is known of it.[49]

A group of altars was found in the theater at Arles, and their original position has been convincingly reconstructed by Formigé.[50] The center of the well-preserved marble pavement of the orchestra is marked by a rectangular stone, rougher than the surrounding marble, with a hole in the middle eight inches square and one foot deep, strongly suggesting the traces of the *thymele* in the theater of Dionysos in Athens.[51] The altar which fits this stone as a base is a rectangular one, about two and one-half feet high and decorated on all four faces.[52] The principal face shows a heavy garland of laurel with two fillets below. The garland is held at the angles by two swans, which also form part of the decoration of the sides. The remaining side faces are taken up with date palms, which again continue around the angles to the back face, where they support a heavy garland of fruits. Formigé has shown convincingly that the decoration strongly suggests Augustus in its symbolism, which carries many associations with Apollo.[53] There is no inscription. A pair of nearly identical altars are to be associated with this central altar by similarities in decorative motifs and style.[54] Their front face displays an oak crown while their sides are marked respectively with a *praefericulum* and a *patera*. The fourth face is un-

[47] See Giacomo Caputo, "Ara e podio Domizianei nella conistra del teatro di Leptis Magna," *Dioniso*, XII (1949), 83-91.

[48] *Ibid.*, pp. 85-88. Caputo's suggestions of Hercules (=Melqart) or Saturn (=Baal) cannot be regarded as more than unfounded guesses. It is perhaps more valuable to note that he excluded the possibility of a dedication to Liber Pater on the grounds that the available space allows a maximum of nine letters.

[49] Mentioned by Caputo, *Dioniso*, X (1947), 19, and XII (1949), 98. In both cases the position is labeled an hypothesis of Boissier, but the reference cited seems in error and I have not been able to trace other references to Boissier's view.

[50] "L'autel aux cygnes d'Arles et la thymélé dans les théâtres gréco-romains," *RA*, Ser. VI, Vol. XXI (1944), 21-34.

[51] See A. W. Pickard-Cambridge, *The Theatre of Dionysus in Athens*, p. 131, n. 3, and p. 147, n. 1. Also the theater at Epidauros has a round stone in the center of the orchestra which was probably the setting for an altar.

[52] For photographs see Formigé, *RA*, Ser. VI, Vol. XXI, pp. 27-29, figs. 4-6.

[53] *Ibid.*, pp. 29-30.

[54] *Ibid.*, p. 31, fig. 7.

decorated and suggests that the altar was backed up against something, probably the *pulpitum.* At the center of the *pulpitum* a fourth altar was discovered, wider than the others, with its back face also completely undecorated.[55] The front is adorned with a figure of Apollo with tripod and lyre, flanked by panels showing laurel trees. Apollonian motifs also are found on the sides. Formigé reconstructs the façade of the *pulpitum* as containing seven niches, alternately circular and rectangular. The middle one, larger than the rest, would contain the Apollo altar; the two oak-crown altars would be placed in the penultimate niches.[56]

Similarly, in the excavations of the theater at Merida four altars were discovered. The largest and most elaborate of these is decorated on four sides with heavy laurel garlands nearly identical with those of the *thymele* at Arles, with which it also corresponds almost perfectly in size and shape.[57] The front face also shows a *praefericulum* and *patera* below the garland. It was apparently located in the orchestra itself.[58] The other three, two of which formed a pair, carried the inscription AVG · SACR .[59] Mélida proposes to locate them in the three niches of the *pulpitum.*[60]

Another orchestral altar was brought to light in Spain in the theater at Tarragona. Here the front carries the dedication NVMINI AVGVST while the other three faces show simple reliefs of sacrificial instruments, the *praefericulum,* the *patera,* and the *aspergillum.*[61]

Added to this should be two other instances in which the presence of the *thymele* in a Roman theater is indicated by a base in the center of the orchestra, at Philippi[62] and at Tusculum.[63]

The interpretation of these remains has unfortunately been hindered by the fact that in each case the archaeologist felt himself in the presence of a unique phenomenon, or at least one that was highly unusual.[64] Formigé, for example, infers that the *thymele* at Arles was an individual "grecism."[65] Puig i Cadafalch is probably

[55] *Ibid.,* p. 32, fig. 8.

[56] *Ibid.,* pp. 26-28.

[57] José R. Mélida, "El teatro romano de Mérida," *Revista de archivos, bibliotecas y museos,* XXXII (1915), p. 36 and photograph, pl. 5.

[58] The location is not given by Mélida, but Jules Formigé ("Note sur la *thymélé* dans les théâtres romains," *RA,* XLII [1954], 79-80) states, "Au cours d'une récente visite du théâtre de Merida, j'ai vu la *thymélé* renversée dans l'orchestra au voisinage immédiate de sa base." He characterizes the garlands of the decoration as "presque identique à celle des autels du théâtre d'Arles."

[59] Mélida, *Revista de archivos, bibliotecas y museos,* XXXII, 27, with photograph of one of the three, pl. 5.

[60] *Ibid.,* p. 17.

[61] J. Puig i Cadafalch, *L'arquitectura romana a Catalunya,* p. 195 with fig. 252.

[62] See Collart, "Le théâtre de Philippes," *BCH,* LII (1928), 96-97.

[63] See Formigé, *RA,* XLIII (1954), 79.

[64] "Per noi e fatto eccezionale la collocazione, archeologicamente tramandata, di un altare nella conistra." (Caputo, *Dioniso,* XII, 88)

[65] *RA,* Ser. VI, Vol. XXI, 34. His expression is "dans certains théâtres romains où s'entretint le souvenir de la Grèce."

nearer the truth when he remarks that the altar at Tarragona was "traditional," although he does not attempt to defend this statement.[66] As in the case of the *cavea* shrine, an *argumentum ex silentio* proves nothing about the rarity of occurrence of the orchestral altar in Roman theaters, since the orchestral pavement is seldom well preserved and the altar itself is an object quite easily moved by human and natural forces.[67]

For one who seeks to discover a perfectly consistent policy of the Romans in the construction of their theaters, the archaeological evidence presented in this and the preceding chapter, and in the Appendix, may seem at first sight disappointing. It will be well briefly to discuss the conclusions which should be drawn, as well as those which cannot be drawn from this evidence.

Expressed in its most general terms, the result of the present inquiry into the Imperial Roman theater building has been to demonstrate the frequent existence of a material bond between temple and theater. The *cavea* shrine, which continues the tradition established by the temple of Venus Victrix above the theater of Pompey, was seen to be only one manifestation—the most striking—of a Roman tendency which continued late into the Empire to maintain a visible connection between the theater building and religion.

It is apparent, however, that the expression of that connection was not consistent. The fact must again be emphasized that we cannot make sure judgments about the frequency of the *cavea* shrine and the orchestral altar, since truly negative evidence does not exist—i.e., there is no single theater for which it can definitely be stated that no altar or shrine existed in connection with it. However, it seems probable that there were theaters with no visible religious adjuncts, and it is certainly clear from the evidence that the elements here discussed were employed in different combinations and different forms. For example, the theater at Vienne had a shallow *cavea* shrine but no other close temple and apparently no altar. The theater at Ostia was joined to a temple in its *porticus post scaenam* but lacked a *cavea* shrine. The theater at Arles has revealed a group of four altars but no shrines, while the theater at Leptis Magna shows a combination of *cavea* shrine, temple belonging to the *porticus post scaenam*, and altar. The reasons behind such variations, as well as variations in the form of the *cavea* shrine itself, are not apparent, but one would be mistaken to insist on consistency when the evidence does not support it.

The question must arise as to what divinities were honored in connection with these theaters, and here one is likewise forced to admit a lack of consistency in the Roman practice. The titulary divinity is known for only a small portion of the *cavea*

---

[66] *L'arquitectura romana a Catalunya*, p. 195.

[67] For completeness one must add the evidence from the theater in the Syrian sanctuary at Delos, although its specialized use places it in a category apart from the regular "secular" theater. Bases for both a "throne" and an altar were found in the area corresponding to an ordinary theater's orchestra. See above, Chap. IV, n. 34.

shrines, yielding the names of Venus, Ceres, and Apollo. It may be noted however that the Imperial cult enters into the religious paraphernalia of the theater building in a rather high proportion. This seems natural, since the theater as a gathering place for large numbers of people would be an obvious propaganda site. As in the case of the theater of Pompey, the religious element is here simultaneously political.

Inquiries as to the "sincerity" of the religious expression here dealt with lie outside the scope of archaeological investigation. It has been the concern of this study to prove only the external religious associations of the Roman theater building. But in the introduction it was shown that the Christian fathers could base their arguments against the theater very strongly on the fact of its connection with pagan worship. In conclusion, two documents from the reign of Constantine may briefly be cited to provide further confirmation, outside the strictly archaeological realm, for the conscious connection which continued to be felt between temple and theater.

The first is a long inscription which records the granting of permission to the citizens of Hispellum in Umbria to hold annual *ludi* independently of Vulsinii, instead of traveling each year to the latter city to take part in jointly sponsored games.[68] The pertinent portions of the text are as follows:

Whereas, you have asserted that you are so associated with Tuscany that, in accordance with ancient custom, priests are elected annually by you and them to exhibit scenic games and a gladiatorial show at Vulsinii, a city of Tuscany; and whereas, on account of the steepness of the mountains and the difficulties of the forest paths, you strongly request that an indulgence be granted and that it no longer be necessary for your priest to travel to Vulsinii for the celebration of the games: namely that we grant that the city which is now called Hispellum use a name from our cognomen, and that a temple to the Flavian *gens* be built in that city, and that in the same place the priest whom Umbria used to furnish annually should exhibit a spectacle consisting of both scenic games and a gladiatorial show, while the custom should still remain in force in Tuscany that the priest there created should visit the presentations of the aforesaid spectacles at Vulsinii, as he has done in the past; therefore, because of this entreaty, our assent is readily granted to your request. For we grant to the city of Hispellum the eternal and venerable name and appellation derived from our own name . . . and in this city's bosom we desire that a temple of the Flavian, that is our own, *gens* be sumptuously constructed, with the following prescription: that the temple dedicated to our name never be polluted by the deceits of any infectious superstition; and in consequence also we grant you the privilege of exhibiting games in the aforesaid city, under the condition, as has been stated above, that the seasonal regularity of the games at Vulsinii should not be interrupted, where the renowned solemnity of the games is to be carried out by priests elected in Tuscany. Therefore it will not seem that we have detracted overmuch from ancient custom, and you . . . will rejoice to have gained those requests which you have greatly desired.[69]

[68] *CIL*, XI, 5265. Treated by Mommsen in *Berichte sächs. Gesellsch.*, 1850, pp. 199ff.

[69] "Cum igitur ita vos Tusciae adsereretis esse coniunctos, ut instituto consuetudinis priscae per singulas annorum vices a vobis [a]dque praedictis sacerdotes creentur, qui aput Vulsinios Tusciae civitate(m) ludos sc⟨h⟩enicos et gladiatorum munus exhibeant, sed propter ardua montium et difficultates itinerum saltuosa inpendio posceretis, ut indulto remedio sacerdoti vestro ob editiones celebrandas Vulsinios pergere necesse non esset, scilicet ut civitati, cui nunc Hispellum

In addition to the fact that these *ludi* are under the control of priests rather than aediles or other secular magistrates, this inscription also reveals that the citizens of Hispellum would not be given the right to hold these *ludi*—which were both gladiatorial and scenic, but not circensian—in their own city unless they also constructed a new temple.[70]

In close connection with this inscription may be taken a roughly contemporary paragraph from Codex Theodosianus:

Although all superstition must be utterly wiped out, still we wish that the temples which are outside the walls not be destroyed or despoiled. For since certain plays or spectacles of the circus or contests derive their origin from some of these temples, such structures shall not be torn down, since from them is provided the regular performance of long established amusements for the Roman people.[71]

In pursuing a middle course in regard to pagan religion, Constantine allowed certain temples to stand precisely because of their connection with *ludi*, which in view of the three categories mentioned in this rescript must be taken to refer specifically to *ludi scaenici.* That this connection could be felt strongly and taken seriously in the fourth century A.D. is in itself strong proof that the custom, observable in the second century B.C., of holding theatrical performances "in conspectu dei" was neither sporadic nor temporary. Five centuries of pure "secularization"—a word chosen to represent the view almost invariably held of the history of the Roman theater and theater building—could hardly have left such vestiges as we see in the actions of Constantine and the arguments of the Christian fathers.

---

nomen est . . . , de nostro cognomine nomen daremus, in qua templum Flaviae gentis . . . exsurgere[t] ibidemque ⟨h⟩is sacerdos, quem anniversaria vice Umbria dedisset, spectaculum tam scenicorum ludorum quam gladiatorii muneris exhibere[t], manente per Tuscia (m) ea consuetudine, ut indidem creatus sacerdos aput Vulsinios, ut solebat, editionum antedictarum spectacula frequentare[t], pr⟨a⟩ecationi ⟨h⟩ac desiderio vestro facilis accessit noster adsensus. Nam civitati Hispello aeternum vocabulum nomenq (ue) venerandum de nostra nuncupatione concessimus, . . . in cuius gremio aedem quoque Flaviae hoc est nostrae gentis, ut desideratis, magnifico opere perfici volumus ea observatione perscripta, ne aedis nostro nomini dedicata cuiusquam contagios(a)e superstitionis fraudibus polluatur; consequenter etiam editionum in praedicta civitate exhibend[a]rum vobis licentiam dedimus, scilicet ut, sicuti dictum est, per vices temporis sollemnitas editionum Vulsinios quoque non deserat, ubi creati[s] e Tuscia sacerdotibus memorata celebritas exhibenda est. Ita quippe nec veteribus institutis plurimum videbitur derogatum et vos . . . ea, quae inpendio postulastis, impetrata esse gaudebitis." (lines 15-59)

[70] The relation between the two is regarded in the inscription as both topographically and logically necessary: "ibidemque" (line 30) and "consequenter" (line 48). Mommsen clearly states his view of the situation: "In Hispellum sollen also künftig die umbrischen Spiele gefeiert werden. Dadurch war es notwendig dort einen neuen Tempel zu bauen." (*Ibid.*, p. 212)

[71] "Quamquam omnis superstitio penitus eruenda sit, tamen volumus, ut aedes templorum, quae extra muros sunt positae, intactae incorruptaeque consistant. Nam cum ex nonnullis vel ludorum vel circensium vel agonum origo fuerit exorta, non convenit ea convelli, ex quibus populo Romano praebeatur priscarum sollemnitas voluptatum." (XVI. 10. 3)

APPENDIX

OTHER ARCHITECTURAL BONDS BETWEEN
THEATER AND TEMPLE

I N ADDITION to the *cavea* shrine there are many other forms of close collocation of temple and theater in the Roman world. In the face of the generally expressed or tacitly accepted view that the Roman theater's "association with the temple had vanished"[1] it would be profitable to examine briefly some other instances where the two buildings are demonstrably connected.[2]

One type of architectural bond between theater and temple is clearly exemplified at Leptis Magna, where, in addition to the *cavea* shrine of Ceres, a second temple was placed in close and unambiguous connection with the theater.[3] In the middle of a colonnaded square, which is in effect an extended *porticus post scaenam*, stood a small temple dedicated "Dis Augustis," to the deified members of the Imperial family.[4] Remains of three statue bases were found at the back of the *cella*, undoubtedly to accommodate the statues of Caesar, Augustus, and Livia, who would have been the three "Divi" in A.D. 43 when the temple was constructed.[5] The temple faces the theater and is on its central axis, the line of the *cavea* shrine of Ceres and the *valva regia*. That the two form an architectural unit is beyond doubt.

The same sort of architectural union is found at Ostia (Fig. 45), where the Piazzale delle Corporazioni forms a *porticus post scaenam* contiguous to the theater, with a prostyle tetrastyle temple facing the stage building and on the central axis of the whole complex.[6] The temple has usually been identified as a Ceres shrine, but the evidence for this attribution is apparently not sound.[7] The theater and *porticus* were probably planned and built contemporaneously, in the early Augustan period, while the temple dates from the reign of Domitian.

A colonnade or portico behind the stage building of a theater is part of the Vitru-

---

[1] See Introduction, n. 1.

[2] Research in this matter is badly hampered by the fact that, even when a theater is published, its surroundings are sometimes not mentioned, and seldom described in detail.

[3] The only publication of which I am aware is a brief statement in Caputo, *Dioniso*, XIII, 166-167, and in *AA*, LVI (1941), cols. 717-726.

[4] This interpretation is discussed, and in my opinion justified, by Caputo, *Dioniso*, XIII, 166-167.

[5] The date, as well as the divinities, is established from the inscription: "DIS · AVGVSTIS/Q · MARCIVS · C · F · BAREA · COS · XV · VIR · S · F · FETIALIS · PRO · COS · II · PATRONVS · DEDICAVIT/IDDIBAL · MAGONIS · F · TAPAPIVS · LEPCITANVS · DE · SVA · PECVNIA · FECIT." (Text in Caputo, *Dioniso*, XIII [1950], 166.) Caputo explains the construction of the temple as purely honorific: "mi è sembrato che, per l'assialità comune con il tempio a Cerere, non si volesse trascurare la famiglia imperiale, tanto più, come nota l'Aurigemma acutamente (*Africa italiana*, VIII [1940], p. 19), che 'personaggi delle grandi famiglie leptitane di stirpe punica avevano a titolo d'onore il gareggiare nelle manifestazioni di lealismo verso la Casa Imperiale.' "

[6] No detailed publication has been made. There is a brief description in the recent *Scavi di Ostia* (ed. Calza), Vol. I, "Topografia Generale," pp. 116-117, 121, and plan, fol. 4. See also Pierre André, "Théâtre et forum d'Ostie," *MélRome*, XI (1891), 492-505.

[7] "... del quale rimane ignota la divinità a cui era dedicato." (*Scavi di Ostia*, I, 121)

vian precept book (v. 9). The porticoes at Leptis Magna and Ostia, however, are expanded from this basic idea, and suggest perhaps as their model the *porticus Pompeiana* on the Campus Martius, which itself is magnified and elaborated far beyond the simple idea of a shelter area for spectators during quick showers. Furthermore they show in themselves an equally interesting parallel with the Kaisareion, the special form of sanctuary derived from Ptolemaic Egypt and adopted in more or less modified forms by the Roman emperors. (See above, p. 54.) In fact, the form of the Caesareum at Cyrene probably provides the best parallel to these two theater porticoes (Fig. 46).[8] It is a large open area completely surrounded by a colonnade and having two monumental entrances. On the line of the eastern propylon and facing it, at a point near the center of the *quadriporticus*, is a small temple, distyle *in antis*, devoted to the ruler cult. The location of the temple in the center of the open area is in itself an unusual enough feature to give force to the parallel, against the standard Roman tradition of frontality which preferred to back a temple against its *temenos* wall. Further weight is added by the positive attribution of the temple in the portico at Leptis Magna to the Imperial cult. The Cyrene monument is datable probably to the Augustan period.[9] All the clear Roman manifestations of the Caesareum are Julio-Claudian or Flavian,[10] as are the two theaters in question. A last bit of support is given to the parallel by the geographical proximity of Cyrene and Leptis.

It seems extremely likely, on the basis of these observations, that one should look to the Imperial cult for the identification of the divinity or divinities honored in the so-called temple of Ceres at Ostia. Furthermore, one should recognize a connection between theater and cult at these two sites as expressed in an architectural complex where the *porticus post scaenam* of the theater is actually a temple *temenos* of the Caesareum type. Finally, the closeness of the parallel in these two cases should add considerable support to the hypothesis advanced above that the *porticus* of Pompey may have been inspired by the Hellenistic counterpart to the Caesareum.

Specialized sanctuary theaters were also built during the Roman period, and we find two examples of unusual architectural form in the Greek portions of the Empire. The first is in the sanctuary of Artemis Orthia at Sparta, where the original archaic temple was "built into" a theater in Roman times (Fig. 47).[11] The phenomenon is described by Bosanquet as follows:

About the year 200 A.D., an addition was made to the sanctuary for which it is hard to find a parallel. An annex in the form of a theatre, 54 m. in diameter, was built round the east

[8] The only detailed description is in Sjöqvist, *Opuscula Romana*, I, 98-104, with figs. 1-5.

[9] *Ibid.*, p. 99.

[10] E.g., Saepta Julia by Julius, Porticus Liviae by Augustus, Porticus Divorum by Domitian (*ibid.*, 105-108).

[11] For a description of the sanctuary see Bosanquet, "Excavations at Sparta, 1906—The Sanctuary of Artemis Orthia," *BSA*, XII (1905-6), 303-317, and Dawkins, "Excavations at Sparta, 1907—The Sanctuary of Artemis Orthia," *BSA*, XIII (1906-7), 44-108; restored plan and section, *BSA*, XIII (1906-7), pls. II and III.

front of the temple, which supplied the place of a proscaenium, enclosing a circular orchestra or arena 22 m. in diameter. . . . In the present case the fact that the seats were carried so far round shows that the centre of interest was not the front of the temple, here corresponding to the stage, but the centre of the orchestra—a point of some importance for determining the nature of the performances for which the theatre was built.[12]

An archaic, a Greek, and a Roman altar were found in the "orchestra" in about the same position, somewhat off center. Allusions show that the festivals of the goddess here were maintained far into the second half of the fourth century, and included a "trial of endurance" by scourging. This, as well as choral and musical contests, may have formed the ceremonies for which the spectators gathered in the Roman theater building here.[13]

Sharing features of the Sparta sanctuary theater and the expanded *porticus post scaenam* is another unusual building complex, the so-called "gymnasium" at Syracuse (Fig. 48).[14] Here both theater and temple are enclosed within a large *quadriporticus*. The theater is of the standard semicircular Roman type, but in the position of the stage building is a quite large temple whose façade serves as the *scaenae frons* of the theater. The appellation of "gymnasium" is a simple misnomer, and the complex is almost certainly a specialized sanctuary with theater. Unfortunately it is almost completely unstudied, the fate of many Roman monuments on Greek sites.

Other examples exist of Roman theaters forming parts of sanctuaries, less strict in their orientation, but equally clearly defined as part of a sanctuary unit by their topography. Such is the theater at Nîmes, now scarcely visible, which was a part of the sacred area built around the fountain from which the city took its fame (Fig. 50).[15] The spring itself was in a hill, and a vast three-sided portico was built under the slope, with a basin and altar in the middle. Facing inward against this portico on the south was a temple, perhaps dedicated to the Imperial cult,[16] while the western and eastern sides were completed by the "Temple of Diana" (a complex Nymphaeum-like structure) and the theater. The whole is oriented by the points of the compass and closely tied together by the portico.

Another instance in Gaul is at Champlieu, in Belgium, where a small theater is so constructed that its *scaena* wall is a part of the boundary wall of the *temenos* of a temple, located on the other side of the *temenos* from the theater but not facing it (Fig. 49).[17] Theater and temple are contemporaneous, and, together with a thermal estab-

---

[12] *BSA*, XII, 311.

[13] *BSA*, XII, 314-317.

[14] There is no detailed study of this monument. A very brief description and rough plan are given by Brea, "Siracusa—Scavi e rinvenimenti di antichità dal 1941 al 1947," *NSc*, Ser. VIII, Vol. I (1947), 197-198. Also mentioned with plan in Touring Club Italiano, *Guida d'Italia—Sicilia*, pp. 565-567.

[15] Description of sanctuary with plan in Bon, "La fontaine de Nîmes," *REA*, XLII (1940), 580-592.

[16] *Ibid.*, p. 589.

[17] Brief description and plan, with bibliography, in Espérandieu, *Recueil général des bas-reliefs, statues et bustes de la Gaule romaine*, V, 94-95.

lishment outside the *temenos*, they form the whole of a small religious and market center in a rural area. There are other similar centers in Gaul:

In light of the great number of theaters which were built in the country districts of Gaul (les Andelys, Pitres dans l'Eure, Berthouville, Germanicomagus, Néris), I consider it certain that there is a direct bond between theater, sanctuary, and *magus* or market. There is no doubt on this subject.[18]

One may also mention Apollonia in Illyria,[19] where the "odeon" is contiguous to a small sanctuary, and Bovillae,[20] where both the theater and circus in the northwestern section of the city seem to be closely connected with the "sacrarium gentis Iuliae" mentioned by Tacitus.[21]

In addition to what may properly be called sanctuary theaters, we find numerous cases in which temples are located near theaters and easily accessible to them, cases which seem to represent more than meaningless accident. We have seen, for example, how the temple of Apollo Sosianus stands behind the theater of Marcellus in Rome, forming virtually a *cavea* shrine.[22] A similar situation is indicated at Lyons, where recent excavations have clarified the topography of the area near the theater and odeum on the hill of Fourvière (Fig. 51).[23] Directly above and behind the large theater, separated from it only by a narrow street, are the foundations of a structure which has been identified with great probability as a temple of Cybele. There is a massive platform supported by heavy retaining walls, which project slightly at the middle of the front, where a hexastyle façade is indicated by remains of fluted columns. It seems likely that there was a system of entrance at the part directly opposite the back of the theater, because of paving blocks found at this point. The chronology of the structure is not well established, and Wuilleumier's dating of the temple to the middle of the second century A.D. is based mainly on an inscription from the area which shows the "first" *taurobolium* occurring 160.[24] He places the construction of the theater in the reign of Nero and attributes to the Hadrianic period the construction of the odeum and an enlargement of the theater. Is the placing of the temple above the theater area at Lyons a mere accident? Two factors seem to lead to the conclusion that it is not, but rather that it represents some conceptual relation between theater and temple. One

---

[18] "A voir maintenant l'abondance des théâtres qui surgissent dans les campagnes de la Gaule (les Andelys, Pitres dans l'Eure, Berthouville, Germanicomagus, Néris), je considère comme certain qu'il y a un lien étroit entre théâtre, sanctuaire et *magus* ou marché. Tout doute disparaît à ce sujet." (Camille Jullian, "Chronique gallo-romaine," *REA*, XXXII [1930], 23) Jullian has postulated Apollo as the special god of the Champlieu sanctuary ("Chronique gallo-romaine," *REA*, XV [1913], 306).

[19] Leon Rey, "Fouilles de la mission française à Apollonie d'Illyrie," *Albania*, 1939, pp. 5-14.

[20] Doboşi, *EphDac*, VI, 316-362.

[21] ". . . sacrarium genti Iuliae effigiesque divo Augusto apud Bovillas dicantur." (*Ann.* ii. 41) "utque Fortunarum effigies aureae in solio Capitolini Iouis locarentur, ludicrum circense, ut Iuliae genti apud Bovillas, ita Claudiae Domitiaeque apud Antium ederetur." (*Ann.* xv. 23)

[22] See above, pp. 22-24.

[23] Pierre Wuilleumier, *Fouilles de Fourvière à Lyon* (*Gallia*, Suppl. IV), pp. 55-57.

[24] *CIL*, XIII, 1751. See Wuilleumier, p. 58.

of these factors is the established bond between the Great Mother and theatrical performances in Rome, represented by the *ludi Megalenses* and the performances in front of the Palatine temple.[25] The other is the public significance which the cult of Magna Mater attained in Gaul during the Roman occupation.

Nowhere, except in Italy, was the cult of Cybele more closely associated with that of the Caesars. At Lyons, the *Dendrophoroi* had the official and envied title of *Augustales*, generally reserved for the *severi* of the Imperial cult . . . in Gaul, as in Italy, the cult and the clergy of the Great Mother depended directly on the sacred college. The formula concerning the safety of the city and the maintenance of its prosperity is nearly always found on the cult inscriptions. An entire population, therefore, is interested in these festivals since they acquire divine grace from them.[26]

A similar pattern exists at Alesia, also in Gaul (Fig. 52).[27] Above the theater and almost touching it is the great three-sided portico which forms the *temenos* of the temple to the Capitoline triad. The theater has not been completely excavated, so that whatever system of communication which may have existed between it and the temple area has not come to light.

At Fiesole there seems to exist a close tie between the theater and the large "Etruscan" temple a little distance below and to the side (Fig. 53). The relationship is underlined topographically by a group of three altars,[28] one of which lies just outside the western *parodos* of the theater touching the *cavea* wall. The other two are near the first altar and at the southeast corner of the temple *temenos* proper. The three altars form, as it were, a series of stepping-stones between the theater *parodos* and the temple.

At Ostia the western *parodos* leads directly onto the piazza in front of the four Republican temples on a single podium (Fig. 45).[29] Three temples—the "Doric" temple of the Forum Triangolare, the temple of Isis, and the temple of Zeus Meilichios —are located in close conjunction with the theater area at Pompeii (Fig. 54).[30] An in-

[25] See above, pp. 13-16.

[26] "Nulle part, sauf en Italie, le culte métroaque ne fut associé par des liens plus étroits à celui des Césars. Les Dendrophores eux-même, à Lyon, portent le titre officiel et envié d'Augustaux, généralement réservé aux Sévirs du culte impérial . . . car en Gaule, comme en Italie, culte et clergé de la Grande Mère relèvent directement du sacré college. Presque toujours on inscrit la formule qui concerne le salut de la ville et le maintien de sa prospérité. Toute une population est donc interessée à ces fêtes, qui attirent sur elle une part des grâces divines." (Henri Graillot, *Le culte de Cybèle Mère des dieux à Rome et dans l'empire romain*, pp. 451-452. Cf. Camille Jullian, *Histoire de la Gaule*, IV, pp. 482-483 and n. 5.)

[27] Brief description, with bibliography, by Marcel Renard, "Alesia," *Phoibos*, II (1947-48), 30-31, 47; general plan of site, fig. 12, pls. VI-VII.

[28] A. Minto, "Fiesole—Sistemazione della zona archeologica fra il teatro ed il tempio," *NSc*, Ser. VI, Vol. VI (1930), 497-503.

[29] See plan, *Scavi di Ostia* (ed. Calza), I, fol. 4.

[30] For the area as a whole, see August Mau, *Pompeii in Leben und Kunst*, pp. 133-190, with plan III. Although most of these monuments belong to the pre-Roman era of the city, the construction of the temple of Isis and the systematization of the whole complex of buildings falls within the Roman period. Piganiol cites as an illustration of the religious nature of *ludi*, the theater at Pompeii, "au voisinage immédiat du vieux temple du forum triangulaire" (*Recherches*

scription found in the theater at Gubbio and referring to repairs and renovations made by a certain Cn. Satrius Rufus contains a breakdown of expenses in which the restoration of a temple of Diana and the provision for "ludi Victoriae Caesaris Augusti" are mentioned in successive lines, which would seem to indicate a close relation between theater and temple.[31]

A final form of theater-shrine combination must be mentioned, although it would seem strictly to belong to the institution of the amphitheater. This is the small *sacellum* built at ground level within the mass of the structure itself. The best documented example is the theater at Stobi in Macedonia, where the central room of the stage building was turned in the late second century A.D. into a sanctuary of Nemesis (Fig. 55).[32] An altar, a cult statue, and two dedicatory inscriptions assure the identification of this Nemeseion.[33] Similarly at Philippi evidence has been found for the presence of the cult of Nemesis within the theater.[34] In both instances the date at which such worship began in the theater seems to correspond to the date at which the theater was remodeled to make provision for amphitheatrical games, especially *venationes*. Such shrines, regularly dedicated to Nemesis, are not infrequent in Roman amphitheaters,[35] but recently an example has come to light in a theater for which there is no evidence of amphitheatrical use, the theater of Marcellus in Rome.[36] Within the lowest substructures of the *cavea* a single chamber, formed by the central sector of radiating walls, is elaborately decorated with stucco relief.

---

sur les jeux romains, p. 137). Bieber mentions that a portrait of a deuteragonist, C. Norbanus Sorex, was placed in the temple of Isis and suggests, "Perhaps he appeared as actor in the sacred performances in honor of Isis." (*History of the Greek and Roman Theater*, ch. 12) One cannot, unfortunately, attach much weight to this hypothesis. The more logical interpretation is that he was simply one of a group of financial benefactors of the temple whose statues and inscriptions were set up there. See Mau, *Pompeii*, p. 182.

[31] *CIL*, XI, 5820. Discussion and text in Moschella, "Il Teatro di Gubbio," *Dioniso*, VII (1939), 4-6. Discussed also by Polizzi ("L'epigrafe dell'antico teatro di Gubbio," *Riv. di storia antica*, XII [1908-9], 111-116), and Brunn ("Scavi del teatro di Gubbio," *BdI*, 1863, p. 230), who states that the second portion of the inscription does not refer directly to the theater.

[32] See Baldwin Saria, "Das Theater von Stobi," *AA*, LIII (1938), cols. 106-116, 135-144.

[33] Text of inscriptions, *ibid.*, col. 106, nn. 1-2. In a rare translation of her name, the goddess is called "ultrix Augusta" in the Latin inscription.

[34] See Paul Collart, "Le théâtre de Philippes," *BCH*, LII (1928), 106-113. Three bas reliefs, representing Nemesis, Mars, and Victory, decorated the entrance to the east *parodos*. "Némésis invicta, Mars Victor, Victoria: cette triade était, à la porte de l'arène, un triptyque de victoire; c'est l'ex-voto d'une confrérie avide de vaincre, et qui, de trois manières, matérialise son désir." (F. Chapouthier, "Un troisième bas-relief du théâtre de Philippes," *BCH*, XLIX [1925], pp. 243-244)

[35] Shrines in the amphitheater at Aquincum (Guido Libertini, "Amfiteatri e teatri antichi di Ungheria," *Dioniso*, X [1947], 103); a second amphitheater near Aquincum (Libertini, *Dioniso*, X, 104; and Jean Colin, "Quelques trouvailles originales à Aquincum-Budapest," *AntCl*, XXIII [1954], 147-151, with extensive bibliography); at Scarbantia (Libertini, *Dioniso*, X, 106 and n. 13); at Puteoli (Charles Dubois, *Pouzzoles Antique*, 330-339; and *FA*, 1946, par. 1999); and in the amphitheater at Seulis (Georges Matherat, "Le temple d'Hercule des Arènes de Seulis," *Comptes-rendus de la société d'histoire et d'archéologie de Seulis*, 1946-47, pp. 9-12). There is possibly another example of a Nemeseion in a theater at Savaria (Libertini, *Dioniso*, X, 107-108).

[36] Alberto Calza Bini, *Il teatro di Marcello, forma e strutture*, pp. 11-13 and fig. 17.

Of what use was this quasi-subterranean area which had a difficult, winding approach, even when the theater was fully functioning? And why was it alone so decorated while all the other similar areas remained bare without even plaster and must have been used only for storerooms for the shops to which they were attached? Might this not be a shrine dedicated to some divinity, perhaps an underworld or river god to whom modest and underground sacrifices were made? . . . Or one might suppose that Augustus, after he had dedicated the theater to his nephew and son-in-law, intended to construct a little shrine for the *Manes* of that same Marcellus.[37]

That the room is a shrine is nearly certain; there is no other reasonable function that one may assign to it. But there is at present no evidence for ascertaining the divinity honored in this shrine. Bini's suggestion that it may have been the *Manes* of Marcellus is attractive, but difficult to accept in the absence of any known parallel. It is much more reasonable to assume for the present that the Nemesis-Victory cult frequently honored in the amphitheater also found a place in the theater in this instance.[38]

Only a first-hand examination of all known Roman theaters and their environs—a Herculean undertaking—could make the preceding list exhaustive. The above collection of evidence from published material sufficiently demonstrates that a frequent and important factor in the Roman theater building has been heretofore overlooked, and it is hoped that such a demonstration will lead to the discovery of more evidence which will make possible a more detailed and exhaustive study of the varying forms of connection between shrine and theater in the Roman Empire.

[37] "A che poteva servire quell'ambiente quasi sotterraneo, che anche nell'epoca della piena funzionalità del Teatro era di difficile e tortuoso accesso? E perchè esso solo era così decorato mentre tutti gli altri consimili erano rimasti nudi senza neppure l'intonaco, e dovevano solo essere adibiti a depositi o a cantine delle 'tabernae' a cui erano aggregati? Non potrebbe trattarsi di un sacello dedicato a qualche divinità, forse infera o fluviale, cui si confacesse un sacrario modesto e quasi sotterraneo? . . . Oppure anche supporre che avendo dedicato il teatro al nipote e genero egli [Augustus] pensasse di costruire un piccolo sacrario per i Mani dello stesso Marcello." (*Ibid.*, pp. 11-12) He also suggests "Dea Carmenta," with little aptness, however. Further, I think little value can be attached to his parallel with Pompey's use of a temple to "break the taboo" on permanent theaters: "E supporre che anche Augusto, pur essendo ormai rotto il divieto, avesse voluto consacrare egualmente il suo nuovo teatro a qualche divinità protettrice." He has already placed it under the protection of Apollo by locating it below the "Sosian" temple.

[38] The list of other possibilities, however, should certainly include Pietas. I am indebted to Professor Sjöqvist for the suggestion that the shrine may represent a sort of restitution by Augustus for the Temple of Pietas which was destroyed to make room for the construction of the theater.

BIBLIOGRAPHY

The bibliography includes all books and articles cited in this study, except the standard encyclopedias and dictionaries, notices in the *Archäologischer Anzeiger* of the *Jahrbuch des Deutschen Archäologischen Instituts*, and texts of classical authors.

Abaecherli, Aline L., "Imperial Symbols on Certain Flavian Coins," *CP*, xxx (1935), 131-140

Allen, James Turney, *Stage Antiquities of the Greeks and Romans and their Influence* ("Our Debt to Greece and Rome"), New York, 1927

André, Pierre, "Théâtre et forum d'Ostie," *MélRome*, xi (1891), 492-505

Baccin, Augusto and Ziino, Vittorio, "Nicopoli d'Epiro," *Palladio*, iv (1940), 1-17

Bertrand, Edouard, "Ciceron au théâtre," *Annales de l'Univ. de Grenoble*, ix (1897), 83-208

Bieber, Margarete, *The History of the Greek and Roman Theater*, Princeton, 1958 (1st ed. 1939)

Bijvanck, A. W., "De theatro antiquo," *Mnemosyne*, xlviii (1920), 122-151

Bini, Alberto Calza, "Il teatro di Marcello, forma e strutture," *Bollettino del Centro di Studi per la storia dell'architettura*, 1953

Boehringer, Erich, and Krauss, Friedrich, *Das Temenos für den Herrscherkult* ("Altertümer von Pergamon," ix), Berlin, 1937

Boeswillwald, E., Cagnat, R. and Ballu, Alb., *Timgad, une cité africaine sous l'empire romain*, Paris, 1905

Bohn, Richard, *Das Heiligtum der Athena Polias Nikephoros* ("Altertümer von Pergamon," ii), Berlin, 1885

——, *Die Theater-terrasse* ("Altertümer von Pergamon," iv), Berlin, 1896

Bon, A., "La fontaine de Nîmes," *REA*, xlii (1940), 580-592

Bosanquet, R. C., "Excavations at Sparta, 1906—The Sanctuary of Artemis Orthia," *BSA*, xii (1905-6), 303-317

Boyancé, Pierre, "Lucrèce et son disciple," *REA*, lii (1950), 212-233

Brea, Luigi Bernabo, "Siracusa—scavi e rinvenimenti di antichità dal 1941 al 1947," *NSc*, Ser. viii, Vol. i (1947), 197-198

Bruhl, Adrien, *Liber Pater: origine et expansion du culte dionysiaque à Rome et dans le monde romain* (Bibl. des Écoles franc. d'Athènes et de Rome, No. 175), Paris, 1953

Brunn, H., "Scavi del teatro di Gubbio," *BdI*, xxxv (1863), 225-231

Butler, Howard Crosby, *Syria, Publications of the Princeton University Archaeological Expedition to Syria in 1904-5 and 1909*, ii A, Leyden, 1919

Cagiano di Azevedo, Michelangelo, *Le antichità di Villa Medici*, Rome, 1951

Calderini, Aristide, *Saggi e studi di antichità*, Milan, 1924

Calza, Guido (edit.), *Scavi di Ostia*, Vol. i, "Topografia generale," Rome, 1953

——, *Il teatro romano di Ostia*, Rome, n.d.

Canina, Luigi, *L'architettura antica*, Sez. iii, "Architettura romana," Rome, 1832-40

——, *Gli edifizii di Roma antica*, Vols. iii-iv, Rome, 1851

Caputo, Giacomo, "Ara e podio domizianei nella conistra del teatro di Leptis Magna," *Dioniso*, xii (1949), 83-91

——, "Architettura del teatro di Leptis Magna," *Dioniso*, xiii (1950), 164-178

——, "Teatri romani d'Africa," *Dioniso*, x (1947), 5-23

——, review of Rumpf, "Die Entstehung des römischen Theaters," *Dioniso*, xvii (1954), 171-177

Carcopino, Jérome, *Histoire romaine*, Vol. ii, Part 2: *César* ("Histoire générale," ed. Glotz), Paris, 1936

Carducci, C., *Tibur* ("Italia romana: municipi e colonie," Ser. i, Vol. iii), Rome, 1940

Carettoni, Gian Filippo, *Casinum* ("Italia romana: municipi e colonie," Ser. i, Vol. ii), Rome, 1940

Carton, Louis, "Le théâtre romain de Dougga," *Mémoirs présentés par divers savants à l'Académie*, xi (1902), 79-191

Castagnoli, F., "Il Campo Marzio nell'antichità," *MemLinc*, Ser. viii, Vol. i (1947), 97-193

——, "Note di topografia romana," *Bull Comm*, lxxiv (1951-52), 49-56

de Caumont, Arcisse, *Abécédaire ou rudiment d'archéologie, ère gallo-romaine*, 2nd ed., Caen, 1870

Charles-Picard, Gilbert, *Les religions de l'Afrique antique*, Paris, 1954

Charpin, Lidia, "Testimonianze christiane sul teatro romano dell' età imperiale," *AttiVen*, XC (1930-31), 571-591

Cianfarani, Valerio, "Sepino—Teatro: campagna di scavo 1950," *NSc*, Ser. VIII, Vol. V (1951), 88-106

Colin, Jean, "Quelques trouvailles originales à Aquincum-Budapest," *AntCl*, XXIII (1954), 144-167

———, "Les sénateurs et la Mère des Dieux aux Megalesia: Lucrèce IV, 79," *Athenaeum*, XXXII (1954), 346-355

Colini, A. M., *et al.*, "Il problema archeologico del teatro di Pompeo e il Corso del Rinascimento," *Capitolium*, 1937, pp. 99-122

———, "Il tempio di Apollo," *BullComm* LXVIII (1940), 9-40

Collart, Paul, "Le théâtre de Philippes," *BCH*, LII (1928), 106-113

Courtois, Christian, *Timgad, antique Thamugadi*, Algiers, 1951

Cumont, Franz, *Fouilles de Doura-Europos*, Paris, 1926

———, *Les religions orientales dans le paganisme romain*, 4th ed., Paris, 1929

Dawkins, R. M. "Excavations at Sparta, 1907—The Sanctuary of Artemis Orthia," *BSA*, XIII (1906-07), 44-106

Degrassi, Attilio, "Epigrafia romana," *Doxa*, II (1949), 47-135

Delbrueck, Richard, *Hellenistische Bauten in Latium*, 2 vols., Strasbourg, 1907-12

Doboşi, Al., "Bovillae," *EphDac*, VI (1935), 240-367

Donaldson, T. L., *Architectura Numismatica*, London, 1859

Duckworth, George E., *The Nature of Roman Comedy*, Princeton, 1952

Du Jardin, Luigi, "Monumenti antichi dell' area di S. Nicola ai Cesarini ('Aedes Apollinis,' 'Curia Pompeii,' e dipendenze)," *RendPontAcc*, Ser. III, Vol. VIII (1931-32), 29-151

Espérandieu, Emile, *Recueil général des bas-reliefs, statues et bustes de la Gaule romaine*, V, "Belgique—première partie," Paris, 1913

Fabia, Philippe, "Les théâtres de Rome au temps de Plaute et de Térence," *Rev Phil*, XXI (1897), 11-25

Fasolo, Furio, and Gullini, Giorgio, *Il santuario della Fortuna Primigenia a Palestrina*, 2 vols., Rome, 1953

Formigé, Jules, "L'autel aux cygnes d'Arles et la thymélé dans les théâtres gréco-romains," *RA*, Ser. VI, Vol. XXI (1944), 21-34

———, "Note sur la thymélé dans les théâtres romains," *RA*, XLIII (1954), 79-80

———, *Remarques diverses sur les théâtres romains à propos de ceux d'Arles et d'Orange*, Paris, 1914

———, "Remarques sur les dates de construction des théâtres d'Arles, d'Orange et de Vienne," *Mélanges Picard* (Paris, 1949), pp. 382-386

———, *Le théâtre romain de Vienne*, Vienne, 1950

Frézouls, Edmond, "Teatri romani dell'Africa francese," *Dioniso*, XV (1952), 90-101

———, "Le théâtre romain de Tipasa," *Mel Rome*, LXIV (1952), 111-177

———, "Les théâtres romains de Syrie," *Annales arch. de Syrie*, II (1952), 46-100

Friedländer, Ludwig, *Darstellungen aus der Sittengeschichte Roms*, 9th-10th ed., Leipzig, 1921-23

Gagé, Jean, *Apollon romain, essai sur le culte d'Apollon et le développement du "ritus Graecus" à Rome des origines à Auguste* (Bibl. des Écoles franc. d'Athènes et de Rome, No. 182), Paris, 1955

———, "De César à Auguste, où en est le problème des origines du principat?" *RHist*, CLXXVII (1936), 279-342

———, "La théologie de la victoire impériale, note additionnelle: Sylla, Pompée et la théologie de la victoire," *RHist*, CLXXI (1933), 35-43

Gasparotto, Cesira, *Padova romana*, Rome, 1951

Graillot, Henri, *Le culte de Cybèle Mère des Dieux à Rome et dans l'empire romain* (Bibl. des Écoles franc. d'Athènes et de Rome, No. 107), Paris, 1912

Grimal, Pierre, *Les jardins romains à la fin de la république et aux deux premiers siècles de l'empire* (Bibl. des Écoles franc. d'Athènes et de Rome, No. 155), Paris, 1943

Gsell, Stéphane, *Cherchel, antique Iol-Caesarea*, Algiers, 1952

———, *Les monuments antiques de l'Algérie*, I, Paris, 1901

———, "Tipasa," *MélRome*, XIV (1894), 291-450

Günther, R. T., *Pausilypon, the Imperial Villa near Naples*, Oxford, 1913

Gullini, Giorgio, "Ancora sul santuario della Fortuna Primigenia a Palestrina," *ArchCl*, VI (1954), 133-147

Hill, Dorothy Kent, "The Temple above Pompey's Theater," *CJ*, XXXIX (1943-44), 360-365

Hopkins, Clark, "The Parthian Temple," *Berytus*, VII (1942), 1-18

Hülsen, Christian, "Untersuchungen zur Topographie des Palatins: 1. Der Tempel der Magna Mater," *RM*, X (1895), 3-28

Jordan, Henri, *Forma urbis Romae*, Berlin, 1874

Jullian, Camille, "Chronique gallo-romaine," *REA*, XXXII (1930), 19-24

————, *Histoire de la Gaule*, IV, 2nd ed., Paris, 1921

Knapp, Charles, "The Roman Theater," *Art and Archaeology*, I (1915), 137-152, 187-204

Kuzsinszky, Valentin, *Aquincum, Ausgrabungen und Funde*, Budapest, 1934

Lantier, Raymond, "La ville romaine de Lillebonne," *RA*, Ser. IV, Vol. XXI (1913), 184-208

Lanzani, Carolina, *Lucio Cornelio Silla Dittatore*, Milan, 1936

Libertini, Guido, "Amfiteatri e teatri antichi di Ungheria," *Dioniso*, X (1947), 102-111

Littman, Enno, *Syria, Publications of the Princeton University Archeological Expedition to Syria in 1904-05 and 1909*, IV A, Leyden, 1914

Lombardi, Maria, *Faesulae* ("Italia romana: municipi e colonie," Ser. I, Vol. IV), Rome, 1941

Lugli, Giuseppe, *I monumenti antichi di Roma e suburbio*, III, Rome, 1938

————, "L'origine dei teatri stabili in Roma antica secondo i recenti studi," *Dioniso*, IX (1942), 55-64

————, *Roma antica, il centro monumentale*, Rome, 1946

————, "Il santuario della Fortuna prenestina e la sua datazione," *RendLinc*, Ser. VIII, Vol. IX (1954), 51-87

Marchetti-Longhi, Giuseppe, "Apollinar, Senatus ad Apollinis e Curia Pompeiia," *RendPontAcc*, Ser. III, Vol. XX (1943-44), 383-445

————, "Il Circo Flaminio," *MemLinc*, Ser. V, Vol. XVI (1922), 621-770

————, "Il culto ed i tempii di Apollo in Roma prima di Augusto," *RM*, LVIII (1943), 27-47

————, "Religione e teatro, l'influenza religiosa nella costruzione e nella topografia dei teatri nell'antica Roma," *ArchEsp Arq*, XXVI (1953), 3-37

————, "Religione e teatro, l'influenza religiosa nella topografia dei teatri di Roma antica," *Dioniso*, IX (1942), 15-23

————, "Gli scavi del Largo Argentina," *BullComm*, LX (1932), 253-346

————, "Gli scavi del Largo Argentina," *BullComm*, LXXI (1943-45), 57-95

————, "Theatrum et crypta Balbi, turris pertundata e balneum de Cintiis," *RendPontAcc*, Ser. III, Vol. XVI (1940), 225-307

————, " 'Theatrum lapideum,' 'Curia Pompeii,' e 'Trullum Dominae Maraldae,' " *RendPontAcc*, Ser. III, Vol. XII (1936), 233-319

————, " 'Theatrum Marcelli' e 'Mons Fabiorum,' " *RendPontAcc*, Ser. III, Vol. XX (1943-44), 13-108

Matherat, Georges, "Le temple d'Hercule des Arènes de Seulis," *Comptes-rendus de la soc. d'hist. et d'arch. de Seulis*, 1946-47, pp. 9-12

Mau, August, *Pompeii in Leben und Kunst*, 2nd ed., Leipzig, 1908

Mayence, F., "La VIᵉ campagne de fouilles à Apamée," *AntCl*, VIII (1939), 201-211

Mélida, José R., *Arqueologia Española* (Colección Labor, Sección IV, Nos. 189-190), Barcelona, 1942

Merrill, William A., "Criticisms of the Text of Lucretius with Suggestions for its Improvement," *CPCP*, III (1916), 1-133

Michaut, Gustave, *Sur les tréteaux latins*, Paris, 1912

Mingazzini, Paolino, "Cagliari—resti di santuario punico e di altri ruderi a monte di Piazza del Carmine," *NSc*, Ser. VIII, Vol. III (1949), 213-274

————, "Cagliari: ruderi di un santuario a Via Malta," *Le Arti*, II (1939-40), 59-60

Minto, Antonio, "Fiesole—sistemazione della zona archeologica fra il teatro ed il tempio," *NSc*, Ser. VI, Vol. VI (1930), 496-513

————, "I teatri romani di Firenze e di Fiesole," *Dioniso*, VI (1937), 1-7

Mommsen, Theodor, "Epigraphische Analekten," *Berichte der Sächsische Akademie der Wissenschaften*, II (1850), 199-221

———, *Römische Forschungen*, Berlin, 1864-79

———, *Römisches Staatsrecht* (Marquardt and Mommsen, "Handbuch der römischen Altherthümer, II, 1), 3rd ed., Leipzig, 1887

Moretti, G., "Serravalle Scrivia—Scavi nell' area della città di Libarna, *NSc*, 1914, pp. 113-134

Morpurgo, Lucia, "Nemi—teatro ed altri edifici romani in contrada 'La Valle,'" *NSc*, Ser. VI, Vol. VII (1931), 237-305

Moschella, Pietro, "Teatri minori della settima regione," *Dioniso*, VIII (1940), 43-49

———, "Il teatro di Gubbio," *Dioniso*, VII (1939), 3-16

Müller, Albert, "Das Bühnenwesen in der Zeit von Constantin der Grosse bis Justinian," *Neue Jahrbücher für das klassische Altertum*, XXIII (1909), 36-55

———, "Untersuchungen zu den Bühnenalterthümern," *Philologus*, Suppl. VII (1899), 1-116

Navarre, O., "Le théâtre romain de Lillebonne," *REA*, XV (1913), 428

Nibby, A., *Analisi storico-topografico-antiquaria della carta de' dintorni di Roma*, 3 vols., 2nd ed., Rome, 1848-49

Nicoll, Allardyce, *The Development of the Theater*, London, 1927

Oehmichen, Gustav, *Das Bühnenwesen der Griechen und Römer* (Müllers Handbuch der Kl. Alt.-Wiss., Vol. V, Part 3), Munich, 1890

Pellegrini, A., "Scavi di Roma," *BdI*, XXXVII (1865), 201-203

Pernier, Luigi, *Il tempio e l'altare di Apollo a Cirene* ("Africa Italiana," V), Bergamo, 1935

Pfeiffer, Homer F., "The Ancient Roman Theater at Dugga," *MAAR*, IX (1931), 145-156 and pls. 11-15

Picard, Charles, "Un type méconnu de lieu-saint dionysiaque: le stibadeion," *Comptes-rendus de l'Acad. des inscr. et belles-lettres*, 1944, pp. 127-157

Pickard-Cambridge, A. W., *The Dramatic Festivals of Athens*, Oxford, 1953

———, *The Theater of Dionysus in Athens*, Oxford, 1946

Piganiol, André, "La loge impériale de l'hippodrome de Byzance," *Byzantion*, XI (1936), 383-390

———, *Recherches sur les jeux romains*, Strasbourg, 1923

Pinza, G., "Gabii ed i suoi monumenti," *BullComm*, XXXI (1903), 321-364

Plantadis, Johannès, "Les arènes dites de Tintignac," *REA*, XV (1913), 434-436

Platner, Samuel Ball, and Ashby, Thomas, *A Topographical Dictionary of Ancient Rome*, London, 1929

Polizzi, Salvatore, "L'epigrafe dell'antico teatro di Gubbio," *Riv. di storia antica*, XII (1908-9), 111-116

Puig i Cadafalch, José, *L'arquitectura romana a Catalunya*, Barcelona, 1934

Renard, Marcel, "Alesia," *Phoibos*, II (1947-48), 23-47

Rey, Léon, "Fouilles de la mission française à Apollonie d'Illyrie," *Albania*, 1939, pp. 5-14

Richardson, Lawrence, Jr., "Cosa and Rome: Comitium and Curia," *Archaeology*, X (1957), 49-55

Ritschl, Friedrich, *Parerga zu Plautus und Terenz*, I, Leipzig, 1845

Rizzo, G. E., *Il teatro greco di Siracusa*, Milan, 1923

Robert, P. Charles, "Les phases du mythe de Cybèle et d'Atys rappelées par les médaillons contorniates," *RN*, Ser. III, Vol. III (1885), 32-48

Rostovtzeff, Michael, *Caravan Cities*, Oxford, 1932

———, *The Social and Economic History of the Hellenistic World*, 3 vols., Oxford, 1941

———, *et al.* (edit.), *The Excavations at Dura-Europos: Preliminary Reports*, New Haven, 1929-52

Ruggiero, Michele, *Storia degli scavi di Ercolano*, Naples, 1885

Rumpf, Andreas, "Die Entstehung des römischen Theaters," *Mitt. Deutsch. Arch. Inst.*, III (1950), 40-50

Ryberg, Inez Scott, "Rites of the State Religion in Roman Art," *MAAR*, XXII (1955)

Saunders, Catharine, "Altars on the Roman Comic Stage," *TAPA*, XLII (1911), 91-103

———, "The Site of Dramatic Performances at Rome in the Times of Plautus and Terence," *TAPA*, XLIV (1913), 87-97

Sautel, Joseph, *Vaison dans l'antiquité*, 3 vols., Avignon, 1926

———, *Vaison-la-Romaine, sites, histoire et monuments*, Lyons, 1955

Schilling, Robert, *La religion romaine de Vénus depuis les origines jusqu'au temps d'Auguste* (Bibl. des Écoles franc. d'Athènes et de Rome, No. 178), Paris, 1954

Sestieri, Pellegrino Claudio, *Paestum* (Ministero della Pubblica Istruzione: Guide Books to the Museums and Monuments of Italy, No. 84), Rome, 1953

Sjöqvist, Erik, "Kaisareion, a Study in Architectural Iconography," *Opuscula Romana*, I (Skrifter utgivna av Svenska institutet i Rom, 4°, XVIII), pp. 86-108

————, "Pnyx and Comitium," *Studies Presented to David Moore Robinson*, I, St. Louis, 1951, pp. 400-411

Strong, Mrs. Arthur, *Roman Sculpture from Augustus to Constantine*, New York, 1907

Taylor, Lily Ross, "Lucretius on the Roman Theatre," *Studies in Honour of Gilbert Norwood*, Toronto, 1952, pp. 147-155

————, "The Opportunities for Dramatic Performances in the Time of Plautus and Terence," *TAPA*, LXVIII (1937), 284-304

————, "The 'Sellisternium' and the Theatrical 'Pompa,'" *CP*, XXX (1935), 122-130

————, "A Sellisternium on the Parthenon Frieze?" *Quantulacumque* (Studies in honor of Kirsopp Lake, London, 1937), 253-264

Touring Club Italiano, *Guida d'Italia—Napoli e dintorni*, Milan, 1938

————, *Guida d'Italia—Sicilia*, Milan, 1953

Toutain, J., "Le théâtre romain de Simitthu (Schemtou)," *MélRome*, XII (1892), 359-369

Ugolini, Luigi M., *Butrinto, il mito d'Enea, gli scavi*, Rome, 1937

————, "Un interessante teatro greco-romano che sta per venire alla luce a Butrinto (Albania)," *Dioniso*, III (1931), 7-12

Van Buren, A. W., "L'abside nel tempio romano," *Atti4CStR*, II (1938), pp. 134-137

van Ooteghem, J., *Pompée le Grand, bâtisseur d'empire*, Brussels, 1954

Waldstein, Charles, and Shoobridge, Leonard, *Herculaneum, Past, Present and Future*, London, 1908

Wieseler, Friedrich, *Theatergebäude und Denkmäler des Bühnenwesens bei den Griechen und Römern*, Göttingen, 1851

Will, Ernest, "Le sanctuaire syrien de Delos," *Annales arch. de Syrie*, I (1951), 59-79

Winnefeld, Hermann, *Die Villa des Hadrian bei Tivoli* (Jahrbuch des K. Deutsch. arch. Inst., Ergänzungsheft, III), Berlin, 1895

Wissowa, Georg, *Religion und Kultus der Römer* (Müllers Handbuch der Kl. Alt.-Wiss., Vol. V, part 4), 2nd ed., Munich, 1912

Woodward, A. M., "Excavations at Sparta, 1924-25—The Theatre," *BSA*, XXVI (1923-25), 119-158

Wright, F. Warren, *Cicero and the Theater* (Smith College Classical Studies, No. 11), Northampton, 1931

Wuilleumier, Pierre, *Fouilles de Fourvière à Lyon* (Supplement to *Gallia*, Vol. IV), Paris, 1951

INDEX

ILLUSTRATIONS

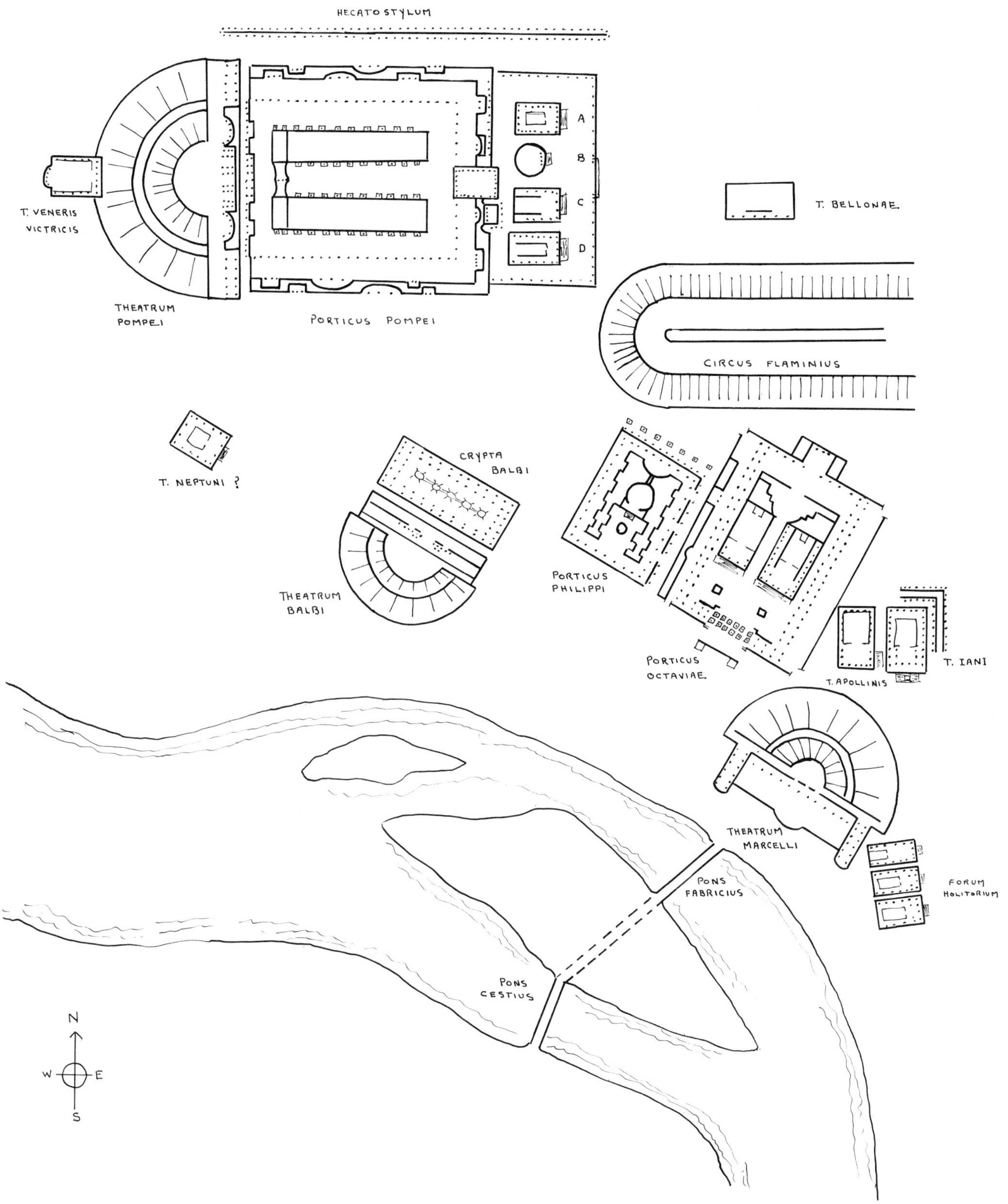

HECATO STYLUM

T. VENERIS
VICTRICIS

THEATRUM
POMPEI

PORTICUS POMPEI

A

B

C

D

T. BELLONAE

CIRCUS FLAMINIUS

T. NEPTUNI ?

CRYPTA
BALBI

THEATRUM
BALBI

PORTICUS
PHILIPPI

PORTICUS
OCTAVIAE

T. APOLLINIS

T. IANI

THEATRUM
MARCELLI

PONS
FABRICIUS

FORUM
HOLITORIUM

PONS
CESTIUS

N
W E
S

1. Rome, Map of theater area (after Lugli)

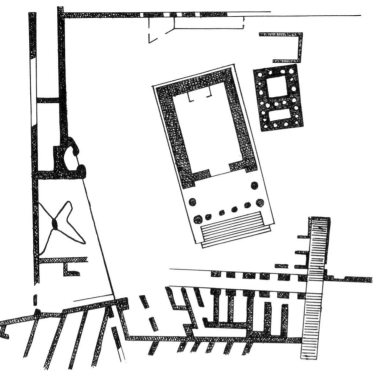

2. Rome, Temple of Magna Mater and surroundings. Plan (after Lugli)

3. Rome, Temple of Magna Mater. Pediment as shown in Villa Medici relief

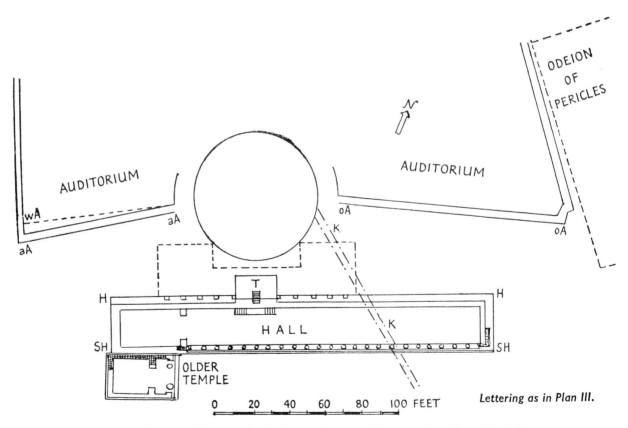

4. Athens, Theater of Dionysus. Sketch Plan of "Periclean" Period (after Pickard-Cambridge)

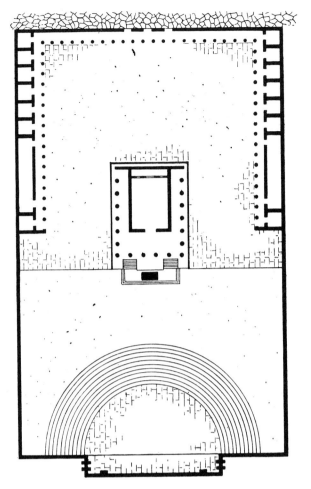

5. Gabii, Sanctuary. Plan (after Delbrueck)

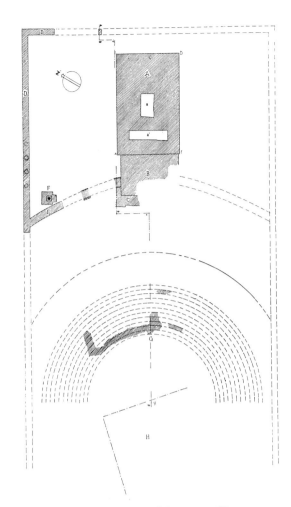

6. Cagliari, "Punic" Sanctuary. Plan

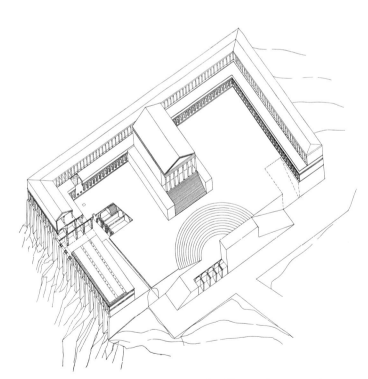

7. Tivoli, Sanctuary of Hercules Victor. Assonometric
reconstruction by Fasolo

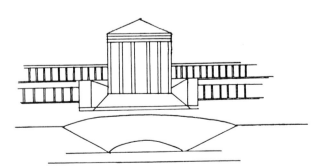

8. Tivoli, Temple of Hercules Victor
Sketch by Fasolo

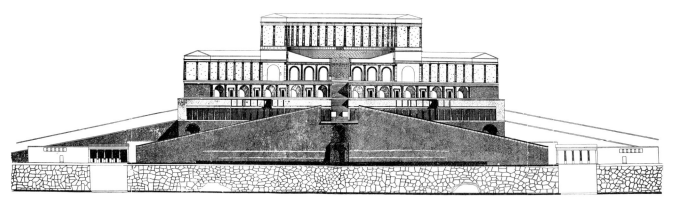

9. Palestrina, Sanctuary of Fortuna Primigenia. Reconstruction of upper sanctuary by Fasolo

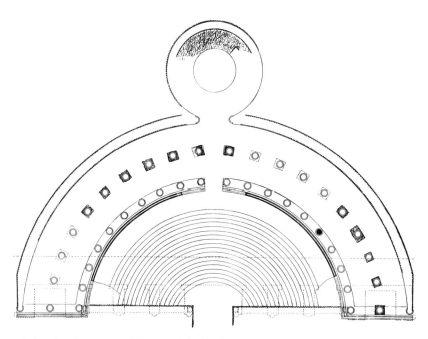

10. Palestrina, Sanctuary of Fortuna Primigenia. Plan of "Theatrical" area (after Fasolo)

11. Palestrina, Sanctuary of Fortuna Primigenia. "Theatrical" area with Renaissance additions

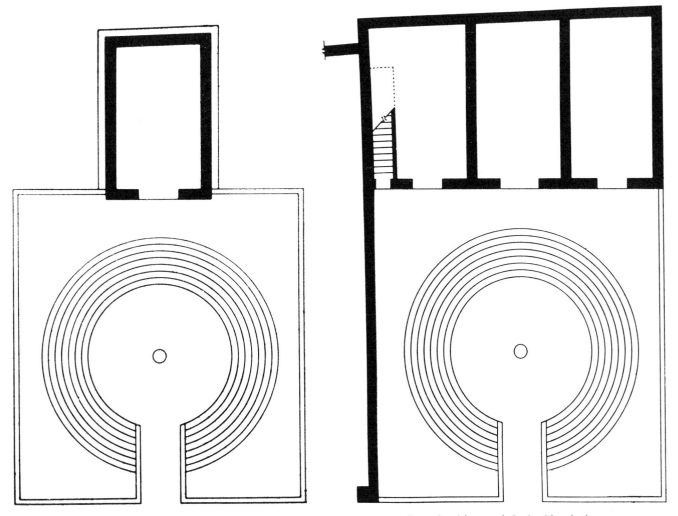

12. Cosa, Comitium and Curia. Plan in earlier stage
(after Richardson)

13. Cosa, Comitium and Curia. Plan in later stage
(after Richardson)

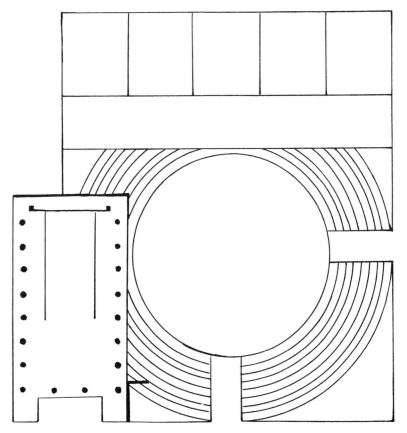

14. Paestum, So-called Theater. Plan

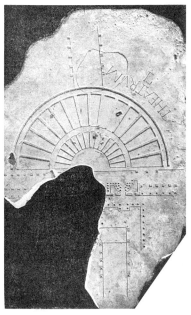

15. Rome, Theater of Pompey
Representation on Severan marble plan

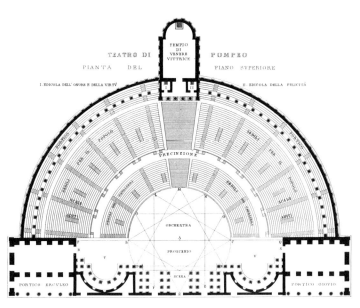

16. Rome, Theater of Pompey. Plan (after Canina)

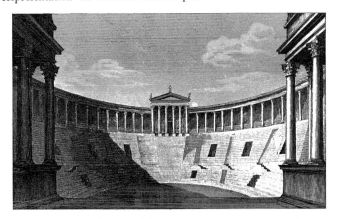

17. Rome, Theater of Pompey. Reconstructed view of
interior of *cavea* (after Canina)

18. Rome, Theater of Pompey. Reconstructed drawing
from rear

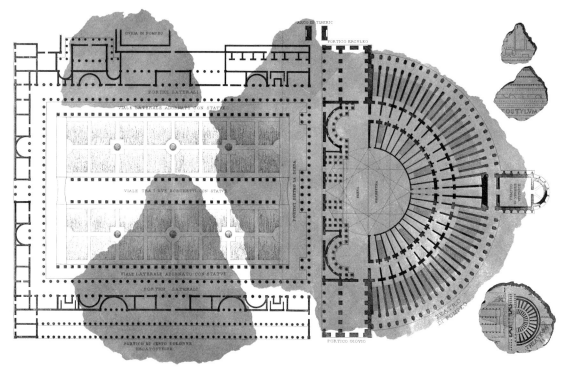

19. Rome, Theater and Porticoes of Pompey. Plan (after Canina)

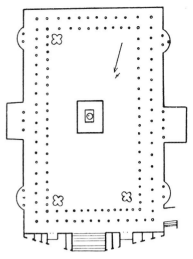

20. Rome, Porticus Liviae
Plan (after Grimal)

21. Leptis Magna, Theater
Cult statue of Ceres

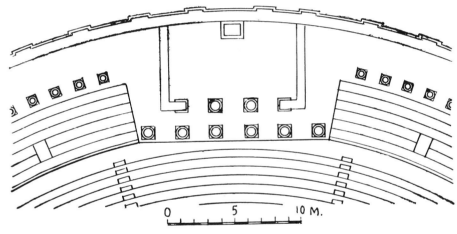

22. Leptis Magna, Theater. Plan of *Cavea* Shrine (after Caputo)

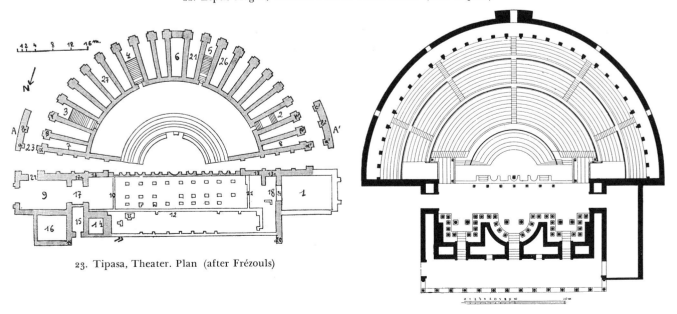

23. Tipasa, Theater. Plan (after Frézouls)

24. Dugga, Theater. Plan (after Carton)

25. Calama, Theater. Plan (after Gsell)

26. Philippeville, Theater. Plan (after Gsell)

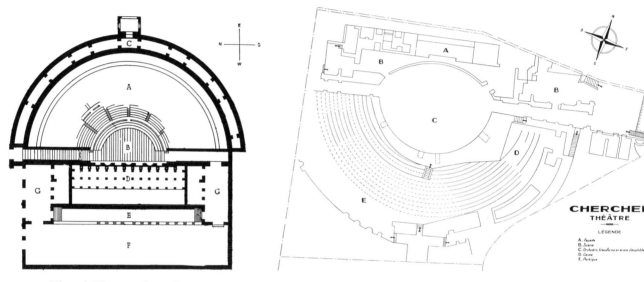

27. Timgad, Theater. Plan (after A. Ballu)

28. Cherchel, Theater. Plan (after Gsell)

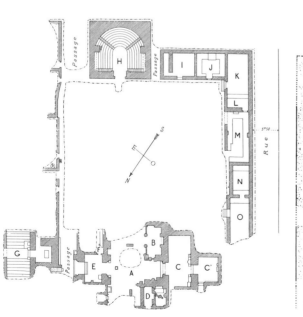

29. Dura, Sanctuary of Artemis Nannaia
Plan showing theater-like rooms at G and H

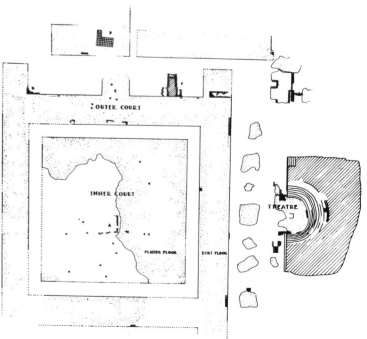

30. Seleucia, Temple A. Plan (after Hopkins)

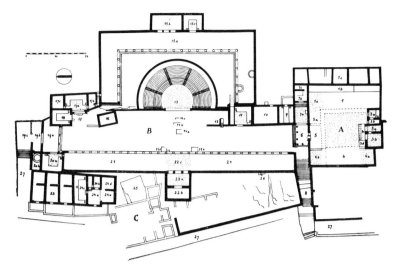

31. Delos, Syrian Sanctuary. Plan (after Will)

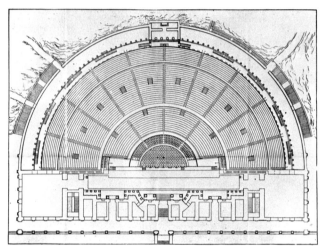

32. Vienne, Theater. Plan (after Formigé)

33. Vienne, Theater. Composite Capital from shrine

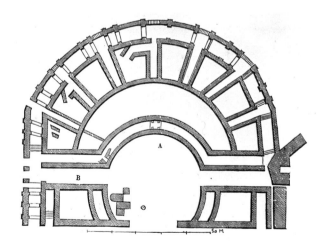

34. Lillebonne, Theater. Plan (after de Caumont)

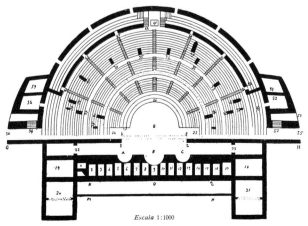

Escala 1:1000

35. Saguntum, Theater. Plan (after Chabret)

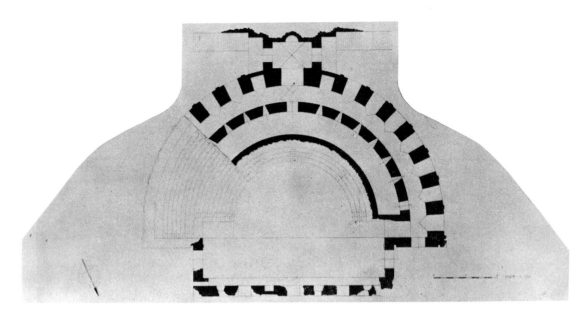

36. Nicopolis in Epirus, Theater. Plan (after Baccin and Ziino)

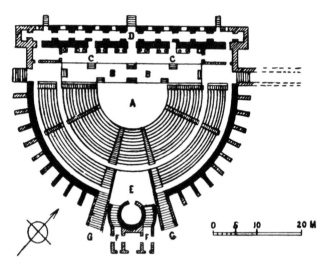

37. Hadrian's Villa, "Academy" Theater. Plan (after Piranesi)

38. Hadrian's Villa, "Academy" Theater. Reconstruction by Pannini

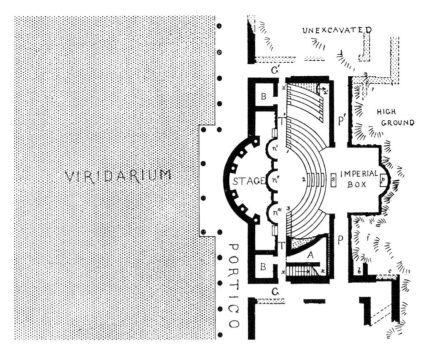

39. Pausilypon, Odeum. Plan

40. Pausilypon, Odeum. Sketch of ruins (from Collina di Posilipo)

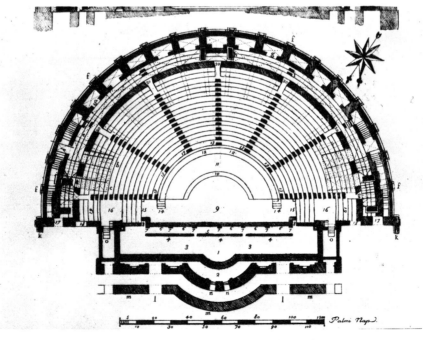

41. Herculaneum, Theater. Plan (after Paderni)

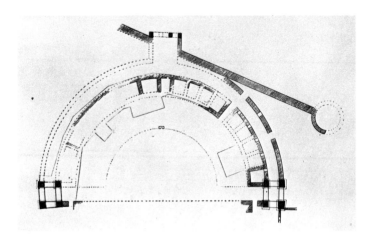

42. Sepino, Theater. Plan (after Cianfarani)

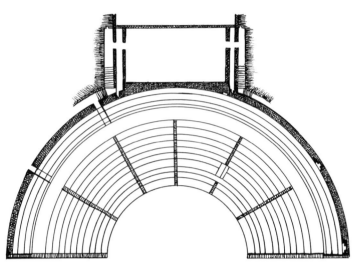

43. Fiesole, Theater. Plan (after Wieseler)

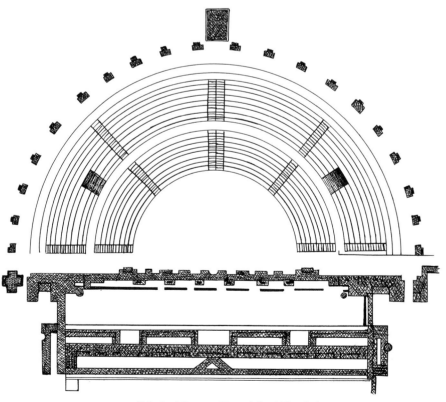

44. Faleria, Theater. Plan (after Wieseler)

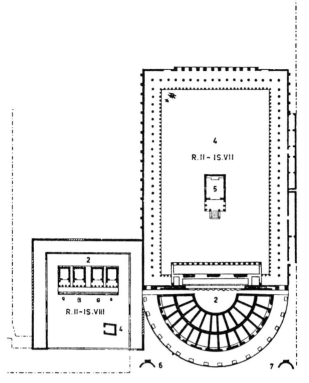

45. Ostia, Theater and Surroundings. Plan (after Gismondi)

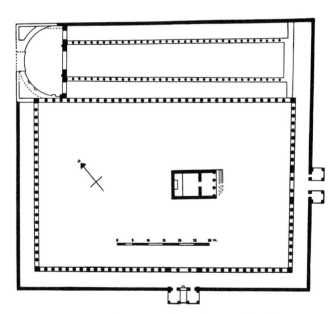

46. Cyrene, Caesareum. Plan (after Ward Perkins)

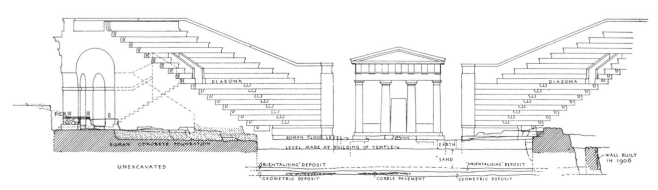

47. Sparta, Sanctuary of Artemis Orthia. Restored Section

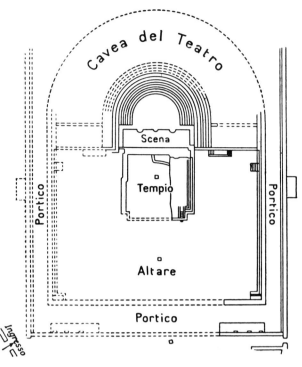

48. Syracuse, "Gymnasium." Plan

49. Champlieu, Sanctuary. Plan (after Cauchemé)

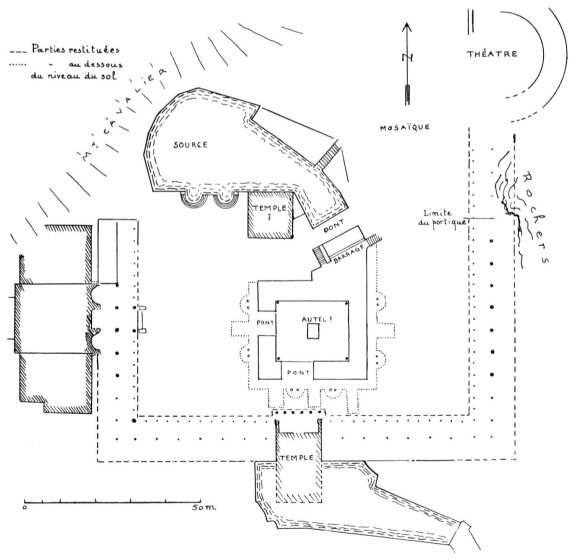

50. Nîmes, Fountain Sanctuary with Theater. Plan (after Naumann)

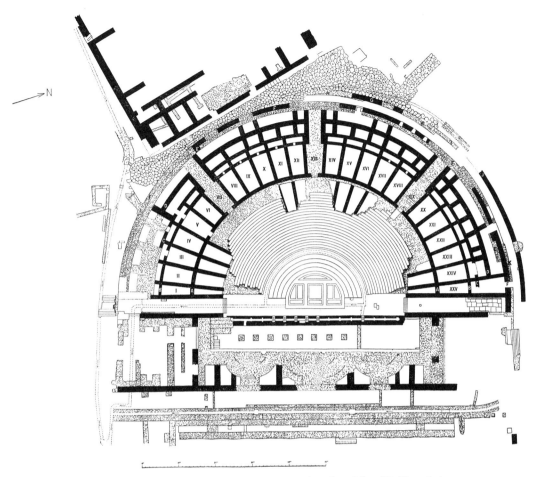

51. Lyons, Theater and Temple. Plan (after Wuilleumier)

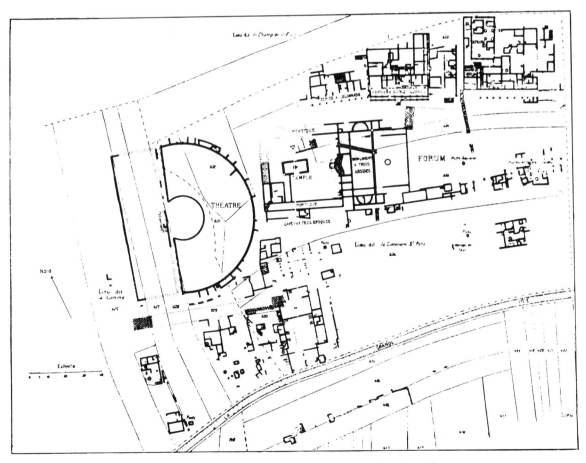

52. Alesia, Theater and Surroundings. Plan (after Renard)

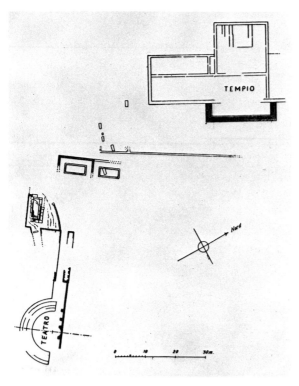

53. Fiesole, Area between Theater and Temple.
Plan (after Minto)

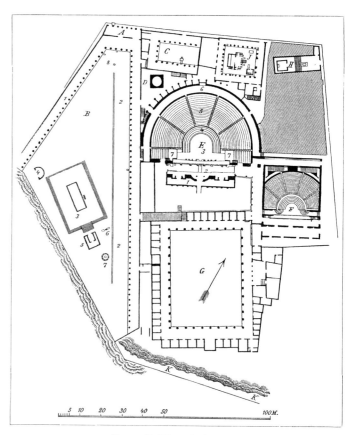

54. Pompeii, Theatrical Area. Plan

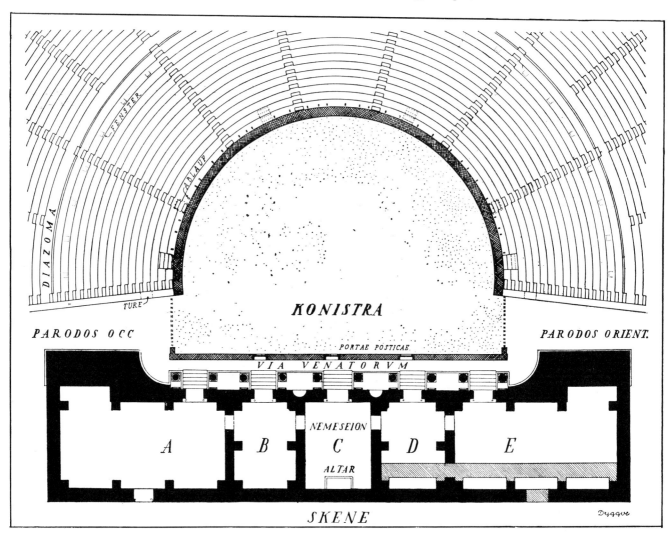

KONISTRA

PARODOS OCC

PARODOS ORIENT.

PORTAE POSTICAE.

VIA VENATORVM

NEMESEION

ALTAR

A B C D E

SKENE

Dyggve

55. Stobi, Theater. Plan of stage building and adjacent parts, with Nemesion (after Dyggve)